The Gang as an American Enterprise

The Gang
as an
American Enterprise

Felix M. Padilla

Rutgers University Press
New Brunswick, New Jersey

3rd paperback printing, 1996

Library of Congress Cataloging-in-Publication Data

Padilla, Felix M.
    The gang as an American enterprise/Felix M. Padilla.
        p.   cm.
    Includes bibliographical references (p.   ) and index.
    ISBN 0-8135-1805-9 (cloth)—ISBN 0-8135-1806-7 (pbk.)
    1. Gangs—Illinois—Chicago—Case studies. 2. Puerto Ricans—
Illinois—Chicago—Case studies. 3. Criminals—Illinois—Chicago—
Case studies. 4. Drug traffic—Economic aspects—Illinois—
Chicago—Case studies.   I. Title.
HV6439.U7C37   1992
364.1′06′0977311—dc20   91-36793
                                                              CIP

British Cataloging-in-Publication information available

Contents

Acknowledgments

This book belongs to the young people who agreed to receive me into their lives and share with me the many challenges and struggles associated with being members of a Puerto Rican youth gang in the city of Chicago. I am especially grateful to Lobo, Benjy, Flaco, Elf, Coco, Blanco, Tony, Tito, Gustavo, and Carmelo for providing me with information not only to write their story but to reaffirm my advocacy for the interests and needs of youth in our society. Lobo, Flaco, and Benjy read the entire manuscript and offered some very insighful suggestions for refining their story. I thank all three for giving so much of their time. If this book does any justice to their life struggles, it will only serve as partial repayment for everything I learned from them.

I have benefited greatly from the suggestions and comments of some of my colleagues who read the entire manuscript. To Joan Moore, Dan Monti, and Jeffrey Fagan: *muchas gracias!*

Several students at DePaul University took time from their very busy schedules to offer their own critiques of the book. A very special student, Ellen Gorny, was forever sharing her views with me about the different aspects of the book she felt were not clear. I welcome Ellen's and other students' comments, for my aim was to write a book that could be read and enjoyed by them and everyone else.

I also want to express my most sincere thanks to my editor, Marlie Wasserman, at Rutgers University Press, for being responsive, thoughtful, and positive throughout the final stages and writing of the book. Her insights were extremely helpful for sharpening my vision of the youth gang. Finally, deserving mention is Elizabeth Gratch, my copy editor, for her diligent care and commitment to shaping *The Gang as an American Enterprise* into an easily readable book.

The Gang as an American Enterprise

They are usually the society's economically poor, primarily Latino and Latina and African-American young people. They have lost faith in the capacity of the society to work on their behalf. Because of this perception of society, many of these young people have organized and created countercultural structures that they believe are capable of delivering the kinds of emotional support and material goods the larger society promises but does not make available to youngsters like themselves.

One popular structure is the youth gang. Large numbers of young men and women in major cities in the United States have responded to their conditions by developing or joining gangs. When they first become affiliated with the gang, they feel they have found in it a suitable social identity and a chance for economic mobility. Nothing will go wrong, they believe, because the gang will take care of all their needs.

What follows is one such story. It is about a group of second-generation Puerto Rican youngsters who belong to a Chicago street gang I have given the fictitious name the "Diamonds." (Of all the youngsters I came in contact with and spent time talking to, only Lobo, Benjy, and Tito indicated not being "100 percent" Puerto Rican; the first two are from Puerto Rican and Mexican-American parents, while the third has a Puerto Rican mother and an Italian-American father.) Like other youth gangs in Chicago, the Diamonds are made up of several "sections," or subgroups, with corresponding "turfs," or "hoods," that are positioned in different geographic areas of the particular neighborhood they claim to have under control. Usually, each section takes the name of the two major streets the youngsters have cultivated into their hangout place, or turf. There might be a section, for example, that youngsters have named the "West End and East Side" Diamonds. Another might be designated "Point and Castle" Diamonds, and so forth. There are other cases in which the name of a particular gang section was taken from a local neighborhood elementary school whose playground was seized by the gang and defined as its hood—for example, "Larkin School Boys" or "Marybound's Boys." In all cases, section turfs are saturated with the distinctive cultural symbols of the gang, such as the wearing of certain colors or an emphasis on certain beliefs and values. The most prominent method for communicating or displaying these symbols of gang cultural identification is through graffiti art painted on walls of buildings and car garages throughout the neighborhood.

The "Streeter and Green Avenue Boys" is the name I gave to the gang section I studied, which is also distinguished by its members as the leading subgroup within the larger Diamonds organization. I studied the Streeter and Green Avenue Diamonds (henceforth referred to simply as the Diamonds) for over sixteen months. I first met several members in February 1989, after having spent more than a year engaged in what turned out to be the exploratory stage of the research project. (A discussion of this early experience is presented in chapter 1.) I ended my formal relationship with members of the Diamonds in early fall 1990, though I still maintain contact with some of them.

During the time I spent with the Diamonds I came to understand their operations as representing a business establishment. The Diamonds operate a street-level drug-dealing enterprise. Several members, referred to as "mainheads," purchase large quantities of drugs and then hire other members to sell them at retail prices at the street level. Most of the street-level dealers work on commission, receiving payments for the amount of merchandise they sell.

Because it is located in a residential area with a high concentration of a single ethnic group—hence, with a strong ethnic identity, customs, and practices—the business operated by the Diamonds parallels an "ethnic enterprise": a distinctive entrepreneurial strategy historically developed and used by immigrants and their descendants in response to their marginal economic position (though most of these groups have established more "legitimate" businesses) (Light and Bonacich 1988; Cobas 1987; Cummings 1980). As ethnic entrepreneurs, members of the Diamonds turned to their network of friends for financial assistance to develop the business. Its capacity to provide distinct merchandise and services (for example, marijuana and cocaine, which are sometimes sold on credit) to co-ethnics is another important feature of the Diamonds's ethnic business character. (At times the Diamonds sell to individuals outside of their ethnic group.) Overall, for its members the gang represents a viable and persistent *business enterprise* within the U.S. economy, with its own culture, logic, and systematic means of transmitting and reinforcing its fundamental business virtues.

This account of the Diamonds as a business enterprise augments other recent analyses that have considered gang-sponsored illegal activities, such as drug dealing, in occupational terms (Taylor 1990; Sullivan 1989; Williams 1989; Hagedorn 1988). These studies agree that the illegal business activities of gang members are in direct violation of the accepted and prevailing norms of the larger society. Yet they view the job of the drug dealer as being like other conventional work. In their book *Growing Up Poor*, sociologists William Kornblum and Terry Williams make the following observation:

The involvement of crews [groups of gang members] in the underground economy is a reflection of the fact that the urban cash economy has become the chief means of survival for millions of Americans of all classes and backgrounds. A small proportion of poor teenagers are entrepreneurs in the illegal sector of the cash economy. In large cities like New York, this proportion becomes a large absolute number. For them this activity is a business. (1985,78)

The Gang as an American Enterprise shares the analytical basis of these works, but it also goes beyond them to advance the study of youth gangs in three distinct ways. First, it places the experiences of members of the Diamonds beyond the conventional "deviant social scene" paradigm and presents a less critical interpretation of their behavior as gang members. Second, the book examines these young men's early lives to better understand what forces and conditions have led to their participation in the gang. Third, rather than showing the gang as a fixed entity, as other studies have done, this book traces gang members' entry and eventual exit from the gang.

A great deal of gang research has been concerned primarily with explaining the deviant and delinquent behavior of gang members (Miller 1974 and 1969; Cloward and Ohlin 1960; Cohen 1955). This literature, as John Hagedorn points out in his insightful book *People and Folks*, tries to explain "why adolescents . . . break the law, retreat into drugs, or become violent" (1988,55). From listening to members of the Diamonds describe and explain their participation in the gang, it became clear to me that they do not perceive this behavior as an act of deviance or failure. This is not to suggest that these youngsters do not know that what they're doing is against the conventional norms of the larger society. Indeed, members of the Diamonds can and do distinguish in their own minds between legal and illegal activities. They are of the opinion, however, that the gang represents the only course of action still available to them and with which they can challenge existing constraints in and domination by mainstream society.

For members of the Diamonds, then, there is a counterlogic embedded in the various experiences family members and neighborhood friends have had with conventional work as well as their own discouraging school and street life experiences. Their personal encounters with numerous incidents of inequality point to a different and more compelling reality. These young men are convinced that conventional society is unlikely to deliver the goods necessary for a better life. Because of this perception, they have turned inward, appropriating social and cultural elements of their Puerto Rican ethnicity and *barrio* life creatively in a way that enables them to experience gang participation and activities as superior to the roles traditionally forced upon youngsters of their backgrounds by the dominant culture. This sense of cultural resistance and superiority constitutes a critical "vision," an understanding about their chances of getting ahead given the limited amount of resources and opportunities available to ethnic and racial minority youngsters in U.S. society today. Henry Giroux suggests that "in some cases . . . youngsters may not be fully aware of the political grounds of their position toward the conventional society, except for a general awareness of its dominating nature and the need to somehow escape from it without relegating themselves to a future they do not want. Even this vague understanding and its attendant behavior portend a politically progressive logic" (1983,289).

The views and behavior of members of the Diamonds have been informed by an ideology of cultural resistance—an oppositional behavior that challenges the dominant culture's premise that respect and obedience will ultimately be exchanged for knowledge and success. Giroux points out that "resistance in this case redefines the causes and meaning of oppositional behavior by arguing that it has little to do with deviance and learned helplessness, but a great deal to do with moral and political indignation" (1983,289). Thus, the story told in these pages is about a group of young men and their struggles against a system of domination whose function, they believe, is to keep them at the very bottom of society. These young people joined the gang in pursuit of economic advantages, but the story goes beyond this point.

The second distinctive element in *The Gang as an American Enterprise* is its treatment of gang members as part of a long and difficult social process of abandonment and mistreatment. Most gang studies begin and end with the youngsters already fixed in their roles as gang members. We are not informed of how they first became members of gangs. This book employs a historical approach, describing and explaining the ways that members of the Diamonds moved from their early adolescent years to participating in the gang.

The Gang as an American Enterprise begins by taking us into the neighborhood during the time when members of the Diamonds were very young to uncover the factors and conditions around which they were being socialized. I look at how these youngsters recall thinking about and responding to these circumstances. From this historical perspective we learn about the positive images youngsters were developing toward the gang.

The story continues to unfold within the school experiences of members of the Diamonds. The youngsters still carry vivid memories of the labeling (as deviant) and poor treatment they received from their teachers in elementary school. The most obvious response by most was to act out the part implied in the deviant label. So, very early in their school history members of the Diamonds were beginning to seek refuge with others who were similarly labeled and were becoming involved in activities such as refusing to do work, cutting classes, and not attending school.

The youngsters' relationships with the police is another important dimension of the journey to becoming a gang member. Similar to their elementary school experience, early in their lives members of the Diamonds were constantly agitated by police officers working in their neighborhood. The harassment led many to turn to the gang in search of protection.

The third major dimension that makes this story of the Diamonds unique is its illustration of the very difficult process of pulling out of the gang by some members. After spending years working as street-level dealers, some youngsters come to recognize that their labor has been consistently taken advantage of and exploited. They come to understand that their work has only been benefiting the gang's mainheads, or top-level distributors and suppliers. As street-level dealers, they have become aware of their permanent position as minimum wage earners. Against these conditions of gang domination and inequality, several members decide to cut their ties with the gang and return to the very same world they had earlier opposed.

Thus, the story of the Diamonds is a tale of resistance against two powerful forces. Initially youngsters exhibited oppositional behavior against the larger society in favor of the gang, and later they turned against the gang organization. As far as they were concerned, the gang did not function as the liberating mechanism they had envisioned at an earlier time. Members of the Diamonds were able to read the contradictions that existed between the gang's ideology of family and collectivism and the inequality produced by work relations. For them gang affiliation has led to the reproduction of yet another experience of injustice.

In effect, in the end we find members of the Diamonds speaking about a return to conventional life to search for traditional ways in which to better their lives. But coming full circle has left them demolished and desolate. These youngsters find themselves lacking those educational and work skills that could allow some of them to move beyond the ethnic- and/or class-specific, dead-end, alienating work that they had rejected in the first place. They have developed a gang identity, reputation, and record, which are used against them by the larger society. One could say that members of the Diamonds are "standing far away from home plate," yet they are not giving up.

One major shortcoming of *The Gang as an American Enterprise*, a book about a male gang, is its lack of information on females. This void is best explained by the nature of the study. Because the study was conducted primarily on the street blocks and corners where members of the Diamonds carried out their daily work, the setting inhibited access to youngsters' girlfriends and/or female friends. One leading regulation of the gang is that, while at work, youngsters are expected to be free of any disturbance, particularly from their girlfriends. (I too was often perceived as a distraction and therefore was only occasionally allowed on the streets and corners.) The basic idea is that youngsters are out on the streets to make money and that any interaction with girlfriends could possibly lead to the loss of a sale. Additionally, there was concern about police busts and the possible injury that girlfriends could suffer if they were "on the hood." Girlfriends and/or female friends were not permitted to "hang out."

There is no denying that girlfriends play a significant role in the lives of members of the Diamonds, yet they are kept at a distance most of the time that work is going on. When I did meet some of the girlfriends it was usually in passing. One day I saw the girlfriend of one member pushing a baby stroller, a young woman whom I had met on several occasions while visiting her boyfriend's house. After an exchange of greetings I tried to make conversation, but she continued walking. My guess is that she was anticipating questions about the whereabouts of her boyfriend or the goings-on in his life—questions that she would not answer.

I did meet several mothers of members of the Diamonds.

What was most interesting was that they all denied their sons' gang affiliation. They were thankful that a university professor who was Puerto Rican would take an interest in their sons—and most of our conversations revolved around me. They wanted to know how I managed to survive the streets of Chicago. I tried getting them to talk about their sons, and when they did it had nothing to do with their participation in the gang. The mothers simply did not want anything to do with the topic. During a visit to one young man's house I used his street name when asking to see him, and his mother was infuriated that I would call her son by "that name." She described it as the name of *un titere* (a hoodlum) and said her son was not *un titere*.

I know of two Latina young women in graduate programs, including one in our own sociology master's program, who are beginning to study the gang experiences of some Latinas in the gang. Their studies will be very helpful in providing insights into a topic for which very little documented information is available.

In any event, the emergence of the Diamonds as an ethnic business operation represents a powerful indictment of the unfortunate underside of U.S. society, the inevitable shadow accompanying a society that is not as open as it advertises itself to be. It speaks directly to the inability of schools to provide minority children with an education that excites them—an education that they can identify with, an education that they can believe in, and an education that will prepare them for a rewarding future. That youngsters, like members of the Diamonds, have had to rely on the business gang to make a living also speaks directly to the inability of the economy to provide worthwhile employment opportunities for this nation's young people, particularly those of color.

My hope is that this interpretation will not be mistaken for a sensationalized, romanticized rendition of the youth gang; after all, the popular media has done a great deal of this already. The mass media, having discovered the allure of "criminal incidents" for its viewers, has undertaken to report them in graphic detail. Because of the mass media, nothing, it seems, is hidden from us. It has provided the population with access to the criminal's menacing intent as well as the victim's anguish. The assumption is that the viewing and reading public wants to see more and more of these incidents and that the more ghastly the stories are, the more receptive the audience will be to the news story or program.

My aim here is in direct contrast to this mass media portrayal of the youth gang. Instead, I hope to provide the kind of sensible characterization that will enable us to begin understanding the extremely difficult circumstances these young people must endure—and, in doing so, give ourselves a better understanding of the complex role the gang plays in their lives. There is nothing exaggerated, fanciful, or theoretical in the pronouncement that the gang provides a mechanism of survival for its members and that, when members of the Diamonds first join the organization, it represents hope and a viable means by which they can gain self-respect and make a living. What we need to keep in mind as we read this account is that it is demoralizing to be deprived of access to fundamental human resources and needs in a society that claims to offer every one of its citizens "an equal opportunity" and which possesses the highest standard of living in the world. Having experienced failure while others apparently succeed, having so little while others apparently have so much, is likely to be a source of personal depression. It is within this context that gang participation makes sense.

I was very fortunate to have been allowed into the lives and histories of these young people. Quite clearly, the young men who belong to gangs are not a collection of psychopaths and criminals. They are, rather, parts of the larger complex situation facing our youth, in general, and the abandonment, exploitation, and suffering of ethnic and racial minority youngsters, in particular. In fact, if there is one message these youngsters would like to communicate to the rest of the society, it is that they are not sick people looking to kill for a living. This theme was repeated again and again by members of the Diamonds, as in the remarks of one youngster: "People say it's all violence and crime; it's a lot of fun. You're with your friends, you hang out, you party, or whatever. We're just like everybody else. If you do drugs, that's your prerogative. But most of the time we're sitting at the schoolyard talking or playing basketball. And that's hanging out. But the other kids who hang out, those who are considered straight, they're not violent, right?—but they hang out, too. It's the same thing; they're doing the same thing we're doing. So there's a bunch of these types of guys who hang out here, and they're not considered a gang, but they're a bunch of friends who stick up for each other. That's all a gang really is—it's a bunch of friends who hang out. We stick up for each other, too. People have a misconception that we're all hard, mean, and that we grew up in the streets and we don't know any better. These guys come from families that love each other. We come from good backgrounds. It's not all violence and crime. There are a lot of gang bangers who are into crime and all this, and maybe they have messed-up lives or whatever, but it's not all of that."

I found it extremely difficult to listen to the stories of these young people. Not surprisingly, they were filled with a great deal of pain and sorrow—the type of information that would no doubt upset many caring individuals. And, in most cases, I felt unable to help them. The youngsters' willingness to relate their stories, coupled with my commitment to writing this book, helped me endure the pain. I hope the book does justice to their experiences and helps to raise awareness so that a new image of youngsters involved in gangs will evolve and initiatives to remedy their situation will be pursued in a committed way.

Chapter

1

In Search of a Gang to Study

"You should write a book on Latino gangs; after all, your previous works, though they dealt with some important Latino issues, did not touch on the subject of gangs." A colleague had presented me with this urgent challenge shortly after the publication of my book *Puerto Rican Chicago* in 1987. After much reflection, I agreed to go ahead with the idea, recognizing the importance of carrying out such a study. So many of our young people were in gangs, and so many were falling victim to the consequences of gang affiliation. Perhaps this study could turn the tide for some, I reasoned.

But what, specifically, was I going to study? I had grown up around gangs; as an adult, I had lived around gangs and had come to know some members, yet I knew very little about their way of life. I did not know exactly where to begin.

Was I afraid to enter into this unknown cultural world? Absolutely. Journalistic and scholarly depictions of youth gang members added to my sense of the inherent danger in carrying out such a research project. These young people have been expressly placed within the context of drug distribution and dealing, an activity that commonly leads to harm. But I was committed to doing the study. In fact, I decided to accept the literature's disclosure of gang members as drug dealers as the starting point of my research. If these accounts were correct, then it would only be reasonable that I set out to study the youth gang in its relationship to drug dealing.

I felt that the safest way to carry out this type of study was by focusing on former gang members. My impressions were that these young people, although some were likely still affiliated with the gang and were involved in drug dealing, lived a "normal life" and that I could interview and talk to them in places at a distance from the dangerous streets where gangs hang out.

With these initial ideas in mind, I contacted friends who could guide me to some of these former gang members. I was provided with names and telephone numbers. Because of my teaching and other university responsibilities, I found the idea of interviewing individuals every week or so to be most suitable. To my disillusionment, the approach produced frustrating results.

I spent an enormous amount of time trying to identify and locate the individuals to whom I had been referred. Over a period of a year I managed to meet a total of ten who acknowledged having been gang members and involved in drug selling. Only five agreed to share their stories; the others decided against it. The consenting five would only talk about certain topics, declining mostly to provide specific or detailed accounts about experiences pertaining to drug dealing. I understood and respected their reluctance. They were afraid of the risks implied in the kind of story I was about to write. Indeed, I invested a great deal of time trying to locate individuals to participate in the study during that first year, yet I had very little to show for it.

In the course of meeting and speaking with these young men, however, I learned very essential information about the gang and its relationship to drug dealing, which prompted a dramatic shift in the emphasis of my research. The handful of former gang members I was able to locate and interview during this period, which I have characterized as the initial stage in the research, were in their mid-twenties and older and had been members of different gang earlier in their lives. The gang had functioned as the training ground for teaching vital drug-dealing business skills. For a small number of them the gang had served as the vehicle through which they had become "successful" businessmen. This handful of youngsters were able to move up to the level of "distributor," or "supplier," wherein they opened their own business and hired other gang members to handle the daily marketing and retailing aspects of the operation.

Another important and related discovery I made was that, at the time they were dealing drugs at the street level, these former gang members had been integral parts of the gang's larger occupational structure. For the most part they were hired labor, "earning a living" through participation in gang-sponsored drug-dealing operations. (As indicated above, only a few advanced to becoming independent entrepreneurs, and even then they were still affiliated with the gang.) The gang, in short, served as their primary form of employment.

Overall, my interviews and conversations with the few former gang members I met during this initial stage confirmed that drug dealing was the leading activity of their respective gangs. It is conventional for government officials, policymakers, and law enforcement agents to define the youth gang, first and foremost, as a criminal operation. In the views of these officials, the youth gang is organized primarily to provoke problems and bring hardships to "defenseless" others. According to the youngsters I spoke to, however, their gang represented a business establishment whose operations sometimes led to criminal acts. This group of young men told me that, as a business establishment, their gangs were under the constant threat of invasion and take-over by rival gangs, whose major goal was to enlarge their own business holdings. They claimed that, when threatened in this way, their gang would engage in battle to defend what they believed to be rightfully their property. In such cases, violence takes on a situational meaning; shootings and killings tend to occur when the gang must shield itself from the threats of others or mobilizes itself to seize a hood belonging to another.

Because of these disclosures, I found I needed to alter my research strategy if I hoped to fully understand the dynamics of life as a gang member. Clearly, the focus of the research project needed to be on an actual, present-day youth gang. Such an approach, I concluded, would be most appropriate for observing and understanding the youth gang in its ongoing, routine operations and functions as a drug-dealing enterprise. I advanced accordingly, having decided that my emphasis would be on the leading cultural and economic characteristics and practices of gang life.

There were other areas I decided to give special attention to. One became the various ways through which the gang socializes individual members for their drug-dealing roles. What process must individuals go through on the way to becoming proficient dealers? Furthermore, I found it necessary to focus on the means through which the gang, in its role as an employer, sustains its members in their specific work assignments. What specific socio-economic environment and procedures are developed by the gang to sustain its workers over time?

The significant role played by ethnic solidarity in the establishment of the gang as a business operation became another major area of inquiry. During the research's exploratory stage I came to understand from the former gang members I met that all were members of various local neighborhood Puerto Rican gangs and that their ethnic background had served as a major ingredient responsible for solidifying their social and economic ties. These young people believed that their ethnic culture provided the basic footing so crucial to arriving at the level of trust and confidence around which business relations are established.

Correspondingly, it became important to stress the role played by the youngsters' perceived circumstances of disadvantage, which they believed were the result of ethnic or cultural discrimination, in the establishment of the gang as an ethnic enterprise. For these youngsters the business gang made a great deal of sense because they believed themselves to be victims of ethnic and cultural discrimination. They explained that the conditions of disadvantage they experienced stem from the way the larger society treats members of racial and ethnic minority groups generally. Thus, the view that these young men shared was that, as long as racial and ethnic discrimination prevails in society, they will be victims of unjust treatment. The youth gang as an ethnic enterprise came to represent an economic strategy with which they would create a niche for themselves outside a system that denied them equal participation. In brief, the youth gang became these youngsters' reply to a system of opportunity they believed to be closed.

In addition, I made the connection of how the youngsters' cultural and ethnic traditions tended to interact with their positive views toward middle-class goals, and, when assisted by specific historical conditions and circumstances of inequality, acted in the development of the gang as a business establishment. These street-level dealers demonstrated an ambition to achieve the same material possessions highly regarded by most of today's middle-class people. The business gang was their ticket to achieving access to property.

During the course of my research, I discovered two additional factors that, although not necessarily associated with the youngsters' ethnic or cultural circumstances or with internal community conditions, contributed directly to the transformation of the youth gang into a business enterprise. One was the enactment of a piece of state legislation that carried severe penalties for adults who were apprehended for selling drugs. With the passing of this law, adults, who for the most part had controlled street-level drug dealing and distribution, began employing youngsters for the day-to-day operations of their business. It was widely recognized that the newly enacted law exempted youngsters who were sixteen years and younger; therefore, these young people became the most suitable pool of workers for street-level dealing. Additionally, leaders of youth gangs came to recognize this loophole in the law and began forming their own drug-dealing operations and employed their own members as street-level dealers. The second factor that stimulated the growth of the youth gang into a business establishment was the widespread demand for and use of cocaine and marijuana. The "drug craze" of the 1970s, a great deal of which carried into the 1980s, served strongly to instigate the development of drug-dealing operations. There was simply too much money to be made to forgo this economic opportunity, as more and more people began to use drugs; it was almost a natural act for the youth gang, which already controlled the streets of different neighborhoods, to become involved in this type of business. Youngsters realized that, by taking control over street-level, drug dealing, they would have a long-lasting clientele desiring to purchase their goods.

As I shifted emphasis to studying drug dealing from within the operational framework of a present-day youth gang, I considered working with the original group of youngsters with whom I had made initial contact. But their reluctance to speak at length on specific topics related to drug dealing was a major reason why this group was unsuitable. There was one other. Since gang involvement and participation for them had taken place during the early to mid-1970s, they were under the impression that most of their experiences as gang members were strikingly different from those of today's gangs. They acknowledged having only limited understanding of present-day gang-related drug dealing. The following comments by one former gang member were representative: "In my day, we used to do it this way, but the gang has changed a great deal in the last years. Kids today are different and do things differently. I can't believe the things they do. Where do they get all this money to buy drugs? We had to scrounge around real hard to come up with the bread to buy a few ounces. These guys have what they want and what they need all the time. Another thing is that I don't think that they are afraid to get busted, they're always out there."

Although the year I spent locating and interviewing this small number of youngsters might be considered wasted, insofar as I was not being able to obtain the kind of information I had hoped to secure, from a different point of view I found it to be well-spent and fruitful. It was through this initial experience that the direct relationship between the gang and "making money" was firmly established for me, a reality that has finally gained public recognition in the last several years. Additionally, I stumbled onto a view of the monopolistic control the youth gang has over the street-level, local neighborhood drug-dealing scene. Street blocks and corners in the neighborhood where the Diamonds have carved out several turfs, or hoods, for example, have been developed as specific "open-business markets" by different gang sections. For youngsters not belonging to a gang section, these areas are unavailable for business. Not belonging to a gang means having to find or create business stations that do not compete with the gang-controlled hood, or market. Given the sweeping control of local neighborhoods by the various gangs, this is very difficult, if not impossible. In essence, this initial period of exploration gave me enough basic information about the youth gang to enable me to begin formulating specific ideas for what would become the next phase of my study.

Indeed, I walked away from this early experience feeling more knowledgeable and capable of engaging in constructive conversations with gang members, though my understanding grew considerably during the following period of research. This primary body of knowledge allowed me to begin my relationship with members of the Diamonds from a "point of strength." Because I sounded as if I knew what I was talking about, the youngsters saw in me someone with whom they felt secure and could talk. On many occasions they would reiterate the fear and distrust they tend to feel toward "adults" and "outsiders," whose typical approach is to pretend not to know some very obvious things about the gang's activities. Youngsters are very suspicious of such individuals, believing they can see through their artificiality. The young people see these individuals as interested only in securing information with which to further cripple their situation or damage their reputations. Strangers are not to be trusted: This is a leading principle and practice of street culture. As explained by some sociologists, because gang members tend to be very suspicious of outsiders, they develop secretive and manipulative techniques to protect their group from infiltration and arrest (Adler and Adler 1980; Moore 1978; Carey 1968). So, while the idea of "playing naive" is at times prescribed as a valuable tactic for conducting ethnographic research, it might, in fact, have a far different outcome (Becker 1963). These youngsters might have interpreted my naïveté with the same misgivings they would direct to inauthentic behavior carried out by other outsiders with whom they come into contact. I used bits and pieces of information I had learned about the youth gang to delicately frame questions and ideas I would share with members of the Diamonds. Prior knowledge helped enormously to substantiate the seriousness of the work I was seeking to produce.

Meeting members of the Diamonds was not difficult. Once again I turned to my network of friends for help. Some of the friends I contacted were staff members of citywide or local neighborhood social service agencies and organizations that were working with youth gangs and/or former gang members. I requested their help in trying to locate and establish contact with gang members who they thought would fit my modified research focus.

The first member of the Diamonds I met was Coco. He was recommended to me by a friend who works as a probation officer and carried Coco as part of his caseload. I had talked to and informed this friend of my research interest, and he told me that he had some youngsters in his caseload that could help. He assured me that several of them would be in touch with me. Coco called shortly thereafter, informing me that Mr. Rodriguez had told him about my study and that he was willing to meet and talk.

I was overjoyed to meet Coco. It was so refreshing to witness his enthusiasm about the study, and, more importantly perhaps, he was very talkative. There was absolutely nothing bashful about him; he did not want to remain quiet. After listening to my explanation of what I was intending to do, he said, "You tell me what you need. I'll give it to you. I can tell you a lot of stuff."

Of course, I was somewhat distrustful of Coco's willing behavior. Was he putting me on? Was he saying these things because he knew they were what I wanted to hear? As I spent more time with Coco and other members I would meet, I became convinced of their honest and enthusiastic responses to me. I discovered that, in general, like many other teenagers in U.S. society today, Coco and other members of the Diamonds have had a craving to tell and share their stories with the adult world for a very long time. In their view, however, it is rare for adults to demonstrate a sincere willingness to listen to their ideas and experiences. The bitter comments of Tony, one of the first youngsters I met, as he describes what he believes to be adults' vulgar insensitivity toward young people, best capture the youngsters' urges to be heard.

Tony: I remember on many occasions my father would say to me, 'OK, Tony, let's have a conversation,' and you know what? He would be the only one to talk. You see, adults want you to think of them as authority figures that must be respected because they are adults and are supposed to know it all. That's one main reason I don't respect adults—I don't respect authority figures.

Felix: Well, I'm an adult. Why do you talk to me?

Tony: You're different. You were up front. You came in and told me from the beginning what you were all about, the things you wanted to get from me and the other guys. So we did the initial interview, and now we are like friends. Other people try becoming your friends first as a way to get what they want. Another thing is that when we talk you listen.

Felix: What do you mean by that?

Tony: I always say more than what you say. You sit there listening to me; you know, you talk but you also listen. I like that because I get a chance to tell someone like yourself, a professor, someone who is really important, things about my life, and you seem to care.

It also was the case that Coco was questioning my commitment to spending time with him and his friends. Several times he said, "You know, we have seen cats like you. You come to the neighborhood for a little while, and then you leave. You're going to get tired of us. You're not going to understand us because we are not like you. And you probably want us to be like that. So, yes, you're probably going to space out on us." I had to demonstrate to Coco and the other youngsters I would meet later that I had a sincere interest in learning about them. I needed to show them that I was committed to spending as much time as necessary with them and that I could even become someone they would trust.

Coco's behavior remained constant: The whole time we spent together he talked endlessly. How wonderful! Conducting interviews with him was extremely effortless for he would speak ahead of my questions. After our initial contact I conducted an interview with him which lasted over three hours. We then spent the remainder of the day talking and visiting his neighborhood. That same day he introduced me to Elf, Blanco, Tony, and several other friends, all of whom were members of the Diamonds. Like Coco, these youngsters were amenable to the study and to my doing interviews with them. All four became my key informants; their efforts were invaluable to the study because they vouched for my trustworthiness and reliability as a friend who could be spoken to.

Almost a year after meeting Coco, Elf, Blanco, and Tony I met a couple of other members of the Diamonds who were attending an alternative high school program. The principal of the school, also a friend, was very helpful in identifying these young men and provided me with time and space in the school building to talk to them. From this program I met and spoke to Tito, Lobo, and Flaco. Lobo had just gotten out of the gang. Tito and Flaco were still affiliated with the Streeter and Green Avenue Diamonds, though they claimed to not have any official association. And, like Coco, Flaco came to play the role of a key informant. Through Flaco I met other Diamonds, none of whom were enrolled in this school program.

Having developed this relationship of researcher/informant with these young men was of major consequence because, even though I shared the same ethnic background and some of the experiences of growing up in a Puerto Rican *barrio* (neighborhood) in Chicago and had acquired a base of preliminary information on the youth gang, gaining accessibility and trustworthiness with other gang members still posed problems. To most I was still an outsider, even though I regarded myself as "one of them."

My key informants also contributed enormously to the study by evaluating some of the information provided by other youngsters. In these cases, I would simply present the key informants with material given to me by others, soliciting their reactions and comments. They would reply by indicating the accuracy and, at times, ambiguity of the information provided.

In my view, I had established not only friendships with these young people but also a cooperative relationship as a "research team," notwithstanding the distance required for preserving my identity and role as a sociologist. I tried making this group of youngsters feel like a real part of the research effort. I consulted with them. I often asked their opinions about different issues or information that would come up in the course of the research. It became common to hear some tell their friends: "We are working on a book about us. We are helping Felix to write our story." Rightly so, members of the Diamonds claimed ownership of the book. It was as much their book as it was mine, and I frequently reminded them of this fact.

The information I sought from all of these young people was geared at emphasizing two major related areas. The first had to do with their history with the gang: How long had they been members of the gang? What were their reasons for joining? What were the major changes in their attitudes toward the gang, if any, and what were the reasons for these changes? What were their actual uses of the gang—that is, how did the gang develop into an agent of employment and social upgrading? What types of money-making activities were they involved in as members of the gang? How did they learn to perform these activities? What are the differences between working "for the gang" and "for oneself"? What were the relations existing among gang members and with rival gangs? What was their relationship with the police? The second area in which I sought information was the mobility aspirations of the youngsters over time: What were their hopes and outlook for the future? How were these aspirations formed and changed? What was the relationship between the youngsters' aspirations and gang participation?

I developed and pursued my inquiries from an interactionist point of view in order to discover both the nature of the youngsters' patterns of shared behavior and their causes. My aim was to learn about the historical process through which the youngsters' behavior had been cultivated. I was not so concerned, for example, with a youngsters's achievement level in school or whether he liked the subject matter. My focus was on how he related to his teachers, his counselor, his principal, and his friends and classmates and how he interpreted their behavior and defined their interactions with him. I was concerned with the meaning these encounters had for him—for example, the way a youngster might or might not decide to carry out an individual or collective course of action because he feels it corresponds with behavior expected of him.

This study is based on life history, or biographic, interviews I conducted with all the youngsters combined with limited participant observation. The life history method was meant to encourage members of the Diamonds to speak at some length about certain elements of their lives, ranging from elementary school to present-time experiences. I also hoped to generate information from the life history interviews that would help to identify and learn about *barrio* features and processes as well as about the influence of significant others (parents, aunts, uncles, siblings, friends of the family, neighbors, and teachers), which combine to shape the thinking and actions of these youngsters over time. While the life history interviews were geared to solicit answers to the questions already noted, they were also useful in throwing light on those forces of domination and constraint the youngsters have had to struggle against in their pursuit of economic and social advancement. What forces do the youngsters believe have prevented them from getting ahead? What were their opinions about why these things were happening to them? How did they respond? In addition, information obtained from the youngsters' personal histories was used to understand the way their gang was initially developed and later transformed into a business enterprise. In other words, I wanted to learn from members of the Diamonds the circumstances that had influenced a change in the direction of the gang, transforming it from a criminal organization into a major mechanism for making a living.

Most of the interviews were tape-recorded with an unstructured, open-ended format. I interviewed each youngster on at least three different occasions for periods of one to two hours each time. For the second and subsequent interviews I would review the youngsters' initial accounts and responses, looking for places in the interview where I should have asked follow-up questions or probed further. Then I would seek them out, bringing the subject around to those questions left unanswered. In the case of my key respondents, I interviewed them on an ongoing basis, learning about events in their lives as they unfolded.

My role as participant-observer was severely limited by the highly dangerous nature of drug dealing and the "gangbanging" (intergang fighting) affiliated with gang participation. This meant that, in my role as a researcher, I had to be highly sensitive and nonintrusive. One day I met with Coco, Elf, and Tony to discuss this concern, and we agreed that, for both my safety and theirs, I needed to be exceptionally cautious. Coco was convinced that I needed to spend time with them in the neighborhood. In his view this was the only way to see and understand the world of the Diamonds. Yet Elf and Tony countered him, indicating that, though his opinion was correct, my involvement in gang activities had to be very limited.

I also came to accept the fact that my constant hanging out could lead to negative business repercussions for members of the Diamonds. A sale could be lost; a police bust could occur—these and similar outcomes might be the consequences of the Diamonds devoting time and attention to me instead of to their jobs. Members of the Diamonds did not make this assertion explicitly; they did not have to. I came to recognize when my presence was viewed as an act of encroachment on their time and business activities. These youngsters were willing to give some of their time to me when they were not on the job, but when the "time card was punched" everything became business—and that I was not.

As a result, I tried establishing some sort of peripheral social membership in the general crowd, where I would be accepted as a "wise" individual (Goffman 1963). The Diamonds granted me a courtesy membership whereby I was permitted to hang out with them once in a while. Given the relationship I had already established with my key informants, this approach seemed quite safe and appropriate for observing behavior that I would later ask the youngsters to explain.

By using a combination of biographic interviews and participant observation, I was able to learn and write the story of the Diamonds from their own points of view. By using these two methods, we hear the voices of the different young men speaking directly to us, conveying an emotional and passionate account of how society looks from the dangerous street blocks and corners of a Latino *barrio* in one of the largest cities in the United States. Presenting the story of the Diamonds from the perspectives of its members allows us to come to terms with the youngsters' gang experiences as they, themselves, have lived them and understood what they mean and represent. At no time did I consider turning to the "experts"—staff of community-based organizations, counselors, social workers, law enforcement officials, or newspaper accounts—in search of information for understanding and interpreting the experiences of youngsters involved in gangs. Most such interpretations are based on information generated over a relatively short period of time and tends to be based merely on what these individuals believe is taking place. In addition, I did not consider imposing my own preconceptions about what the youngsters were doing without actually finding out what activities they were engaged in. Had I forced my assumptions on the reality of the gang, our grasp of its finer qualities and characteristics certainly would have been superficial and, imperialistic; the actual story would have been left essentially unexamined.

As members of the Diamonds tell their stories, they disclose the problematics of their social world as well as the information we need to know to produce life opportunities for them. The information I was able to secure to write their group story is rich and insightful and serves as an important tool for formulating, publicizing, and pursuing change that can improve their life chances. The Diamonds's stories are significant in helping us to reconstruct knowledge not only about themselves but also about the society of which they are part. The stories can assist us in expanding our own critiques of existing dominant culture's explanations of gang participation and action.

To truly capture the thoughts and impressions of members of the Diamonds I chose to write the story by using the words, terms, and expressions used by Flaco, Coco, Benjy, Lobo, and the others to describe and explain the many issues and situations they experienced. Long passages from my field notes and interviews make up the bulk of the information presented in the book. Writing the story of the Diamonds as conveyed by them was a choice informed by my social and political responsibility to the Latino community and to young people, including university students. As a professor, I have made a commitment to write for the entire public, to make sure that my colleagues and peers as well as nonacademics can read and understand the story. Therefore, I refrained from saddling the story with all the usual jargon of social science. To have followed this conventional approach would have meant keeping the book from the hands of the very same people it purports to empower.

I tried repaying members of the Diamonds as much as possible the many favors and deeds they did for me by offering routine favors. I decided never to give them any money, and, though at times some insisted, I never did. There were many times when I would take some of them for lunch or dinner. In other instances I brought several to the university where I teach and work. I wanted to expose them to a world I knew they had never seen nor experienced firsthand. This exposure, I thought, would stimulate them to consider becoming part of this or a similar institutional environment. At least, I wanted to see if by visiting the campus they would be inspired to ask questions about it, its students, and its programs. These young men were always excited about coming to the university for a visit. And every time they wondered, if only for a moment, how it would feel to be a part of such a school. One young man became most impressed with the prospects of such an idea, and eventually we managed to convince him that he could perform well in this school environment. He did enroll.

In large measure, I tried repaying members of the Diamonds for the time they had committed to and invested in the study by suggesting advice and insights about different aspects of their lives. I believed that this was something they would appreciate more than any other favor.

On many occasions I found myself having to serve as a sort of counselor for one young man, who was experiencing serious personal difficulties stemming from being a husband and father at the age of nineteen. He had just separated from his wife and child, both of whom he loved. I met with him and suggested different ideas for trying to stay on course with the various and difficult roles he was having to responsibly carry out at such an early age.

It was with Lobo that I had many conversations about enrolling in the university where I teach. On one occasion I brought him and his girlfriend, Maria, for a visit to the campus and introduced them to one of our admission's counselors. Following this initial contact both Lobo and Maria decided to enroll at DePaul University. Since their scores in the college entrance examination were below university standards, they agreed to participate in a residential, six-week summer program at DePaul which offered a series of remedial classes geared to improve the academic skills of students like themselves. After successfully completing the program they were admitted as members of DePaul University's freshman class of 1990. In fact, Lobo performed so impressively in the program that he was permitted to enroll in our Freshman Seminar program for his introductory sociology class. Additionally, I hired Lobo and Maria to work with us as student workers at the Center for Latino Research for which I serve as director.

What follows is the story of the Diamonds, one of many still needing to be told about youngsters living on the margins of society. This a story about the courageous efforts on the part of a group of young men to struggle against almost insurmountable odds—a group of young men calling out for society to provide them with the emotional support, human kindness, and material resources that every youngster deserves.

Chapter

2

A Changing Neighborhood

The Diamonds's turf is stationed in a neighborhood located five miles northwest of downtown Chicago. Getting there from my office is a ten-minute car drive. It was a great convenience to be situated so near, for I could be in the neighborhood quickly on occasions when members of the Diamonds would call and ask me to come over to hang out and talk or to do a favor.

The majority of this area's residents today are Latinos. In 1980, 43,829 people of "Spanish origin" were counted by the U.S. Census as living in the area, making it one of the largest four Latino communities in the city. Out of this total, 23,792 were Puerto Ricans, 14,961 Mexicans, and 1,590 Cubans. For a very long time, however, the neighborhood where the Diamonds operate was essentially the home of foreign-born and native European ethnics. Census reports show that considerable numbers of Swedes, Norwegians, Germans, Scandinavians, Russian Jews, and Poles all lived in this community at different times. Out of a total population of 114,174 in 1930, 33.5 percent were Polish, 16.7 percent German, 12.4 percent Norwegian, 9.9 percent Russian Jewish, and 4.4 percent Swedish. The figures changed very little over the next ten years. By 1960, when the total population of the community was officially counted at 94,799, only 723 were nonwhites. In the same year Poles were the most numerous, representing over 40 percent of all residents, followed only by Germans at a little over 12 percent. As late as 1970 the census described this area as a predominantly white community: Of a total of 88,555 residents only 15,765 were Latino.

Puerto Ricans, who make up the largest group among Latinos, often refer to this neighborhood as "Suburbia" (pronounced *sooboorbia*), for living there is perceived as a measure of social prosperity and improvement. Puerto Rican residents of Suburbia do not want to be mistaken with "those people from Division Street," the long-standing Puerto Rican barrio that is located immediately to the south. Although Division Street residents hold their community in high esteem and honor it, the mass media, civic government, and individuals familiar with the area have always attributed to it those stereotypic characteristics conventionally bestowed upon slum areas and those who dwell in them. To avoid this typecast Suburbia's Puerto Ricans, some of whom lived in Division Street at some point, privately deny any affiliation with it.

Members of the Diamonds do not necessarily use the name Suburbia—or any other, for that matter—when referring to this community. Instead, they have developed a sense of and understanding for the different and competing hoods within it and allude to them according to corresponding designations. Nevertheless, they hold the overall area in a bright light. In fact, Flaco, Tito, Benjy, Elf, Coco, and the others are of the opinion that they represent integral components of Suburbia. In the same way that biological organs are inherently connected to the human body, these young people believe they represent natural parts of their surrounding social environment.

When commenting on different neighborhood activities members of the Diamonds are careful with their remarks, for, as they see it, they are offering opinions about themselves. When they make negative comments about Suburbia they feel they are putting themselves down. When their comments about the neighborhood are positive there is a special sense of gratification. It is common to hear someone say, "This is our neighborhood; this is us. I like this neighborhood because this is where I learned most of the things I know. It taught me many things. So I have to be good to it. We have to protect it because the opposition gangs, if they take it over, they are going to mess it up. If other gangs were here, the neighborhood will not be the same. This is a good neighborhood because we have made it this way. There are all kinds of things going on here. There is people out on the streets all the time. That's cool. You know, there are neighborhoods that ain't into nothing. You never get to see people hanging out. I think that they are scared to be out. Our people—you know, everybody in the neighborhood—we like to be with each other. Like us guys, hey, we spend all the time together, you know, outside in the streets, always doing our thing. That's part of who we are, you know, the life of the streets."

Another member explains the sense of community this way: "We gave our neighborhood its identity. You can find our marks all over it. The different murals that we painted, the signs we sprayed on walls, on the garages and alleys—hey, these are things about our gang identity. In every neighborhood you can find these kinds of signs and stuff. In this neighborhood, in our neighborhood, you can find signs that are about us. They let you know who runs things around here. And, of course, we say that the neighborhood is in us. We talk about that, especially when we hear that other gangs are planning to make a move on us. We talk about how we are marked by the different things that happened around here. There are a whole lot of them. Like, we have gotten beat up here. Opposition gangs have come after us here. They know where to find us because everybody knows this is our hood. The cops have chased us here. We have busted some heads here. This is where we make our cash, and that's because we've been here long enough to get to know the neighborhood real good."

These various impressions of Suburbia represent exceptional mental pictures that members of the Diamonds and Latino individuals had or have developed for their community. A great deal of individual and social pain and suffering has gone into maintaining and reinforcing these positive visions for life in Suburbia has been filled with an enormous amount of hardship. Latino residents of Suburbia have had to come to terms with two decades of structural changes, which have left many without (or have severely diminished) traditional avenues for earning a living and organizing their lives. Of major significance is the economic restructuring and its accompanying elements which have taken place in the city and its surrounding areas. Like other individuals and families in Chicago, Suburbia residents have witnessed the virtual disappearance of factory jobs from the city's economy and the coming of a new type of work which requires individuals to possess high levels of education and/or technological training in order to secure good-paying and joyful employment. At the same time families have witnessed the worsening of the Chicago public school system—the very same societal institution that is expected to carry out the function of preparing young people for this new economic order. An additional change involves the transformation of Suburbia into an area crowded with competing youth gangs.

The discussion presented in this chapter focuses on these local and citywide changes and addresses a series of specific questions: What are the essential ingredients of these changes? How have Latino residents in Suburbia, including the youth, tried coming to terms with them? Put plainly, what strategies have they developed to cope? And how have both the larger society and immediate community responded to the different survival strategies and schemes created, particularly those like the youth gang, which are viewed to be in violation of the law?

═ *Latinos in Suburbia: First Contact*

Settlement in Suburbia by Puerto Rican families, including those of the members of the Diamonds, is part of a general Latino population movement toward the northwest side of the city which started during the early 1970s and, which was ignited, in part, by the fast growth and dispersal of Latinos throughout the city during this period. Between 1970 and 1980 there was an estimated 71 percent increase in the Latino population, and by 1983 the total number of Latinos living in the city exceeded one-half million people, or 17 percent of the total population (Latino Institute 1983, 1–2). Suburbia's central, or midpoint, location between Division Street and northwest side communities resulted in the community absorbing a fairly sizable number of Puerto Rican individuals and families. In addition, as longtime residents of Chicago, Puerto Ricans believed they knew those areas and neighborhoods in the city which were suitable for raising children. The move to Suburbia was inspired by that view (all of the parents of members of the Diamonds had lived in Chicago for nearly fifteen years before settling in Suburbia). Parents considered Suburbia a serene and tranquil neighborhood, a place with safe streets and good public schools.

In the parents' views Suburbia was not a "gangland" community, as sociologist Frederic L. Thrasher defined various areas he studied in the 1920s in Chicago, which he discovered to be filled with countless numbers of social problems, including those that spark youth to establish relations as gang members. Simply put, Puerto Rican parents knew that Suburbia was not a city slum or a rundown neighborhood. They were convinced that in this area their children could best pursue and achieve the individual and social advancement that they themselves were not able to realize.

Superior Housing Quality

Anyone who takes a casual walk through some of Suburbia's street blocks today could understand why Puerto Rican and other Latino families assigned the community such high appraisal twenty years ago and still do. One of the most noticeable features of Suburbia is its housing. It is unquestionably splendid—of high quality and aesthetic style.

Suburbia is one of the original "boulevard communities" of the city; as such, some of its housing clearly is characteristic of this unique system. The boulevards were once the choice sites of prosperous merchants and entrepreneurs, who built magnificent mansions in the city. Resembling a green necklace of open space sparkling with trees, monuments, fountains, parks, and landscaped squares, the boulevard system represents continuous wide, landscaped thoroughfares (modeled after the grand Parisian boulevards) which pass through approximately thirty-four communities in Chicago and cover a total of twenty-eight miles. A recent report by the city's department of planning suggests that the city's boulevard system "should be as closely linked with the name 'Chicago' as Central Park is to New York, the hills to Hollywood, or our own lakefront and skyline to Chicago" (1989, 5).

Lining Suburbia's two boulevards and its major square are "late-Victorian and Queen Anne–style mansions bedecked with towers, turrets, classical columns, bays, stained glass and balustrades" (Chicago House Hunt Book 1989, 50). The most popular residence is the two-flat graystone with three bedrooms and one bath per unit.

A housing-building boom during the late 1920s established Suburbia as a "rental area," with most of its residential units contained in two- and three-unit flats and a small proportion (less than 20 percent) in apartment buildings of ten or more units. Suburbia's housing makeup has changed very little over time. In 1940, 75.1 percent of the housing was tenant-occupied. Census reports for the twenty-year period between 1950 and 1970 showed essentially the same numbers. The count for 1980 was

65.1 percent. Overall, Suburbia has sustained itself as a hub for tenant families and individuals.

The sharp increase in the price of housing experienced in most U.S. cities during the 1980s pushed up the price of housing in Suburbia. By spring 1990, two- and three-unit properties on the boulevards and square were selling for a minimum of $200,000 up to $350,000. On side streets two-unit flats were going for $100,000 to $200,000. Until recent times, however, most of Suburbia's housing was relatively inexpensive and affordable. In 1960, for example, the median value for owner-occupied units was $13,700. Twenty years later the census reports showed a moderate increase, to a median value of $30,460, roughly one-third less than the city average.

Working-Class Community

The job situation of Suburbia residents over time served as further confirmation for the positive views and high appraisal Puerto Ricans expressed for the area. Puerto Ricans arrived in Suburbia and joined a community where working-class people resided alongside those employed in white-collar professional occupations. (During the 1980s a large number of young urban professionals moved into the area. Attracted by Suburbia's reputable housing stock and its close proximity to downtown, many purchased and rehabilitated some of the best housing in Suburbia.)

Suburbia's healthy economic profile reflects the overall economic situation of Chicago. The "city with big shoulders" became a popular slogan used to describe Chicago in reference to its development as the economic fortress of the Midwest and, indeed, as one of the leading industrial manufacturing centers of the nation. For most of its long history of economic growth Chicago offered numerous job opportunities to hundreds of thousands of new arrivals in many of its wide-ranging manufacturing sector. Beginning in the latter part of the nineteenth century and continuing for the next fifty years, steel mills, freight warehouses, meat-packing houses, mail-order establishments, construction projects, clothing shops, breweries, distilleries, and a host of complementary industries that serviced factories or utilized their byproducts were the leading centers of employment in the city of Chicago.

The founding and growth of Chicago's manufacturing economy was greatly aided by its key location on Lake Michigan and its development as the center of a regional and, later, national railroad system—both of which combined to make Chicago one of the primary centers of transportation in the country. Just as important, the increasing growth in population and its attendant surplus of labor contributed directly to the development and maintenance of Chicago's industrial manufacturing economy. Like other industrial cities, Chicago's burgeoning factory system revolved around a continual availability of a "reserve army" of workers—workers who could be mobilized during periods of economic expansion and laid off during periods of economic decline without serious social disruption. In fact, this reserve army of workers helped to discipline those inside the factory gates; their availability served as a constant reminder to permanent workers that they could easily be replaced. Indeed, being second only to New York, the "Great Metropolis," in terms of economic and population growth, Chicago received a massive share of workers.

For Suburbia and other city residents to find employment in Chicago's manufacturing economy they simply needed to demonstrate a willingness and desire to work. Lack of educational credentials, special job training, or English fluency did not represent obstacles for incorporation into the work force at this time. In effect, the rapidly expanding industrial urban economy, characterized by an abundance of entry-level jobs and with few requisites for entry, could not afford to turn away prospective laborers. In 1940, when the median school years completed for Suburbia's residents was 8.2, the unemployment rate for a labor force of 53,174 was a little over 5 percent. By 1960, on the other hand, when the median school years completed had increased moderately to 9.1, the unemployment rate had dropped to 4.2 percent.

To be sure, industrial manufacturing Chicago was filled with an abundance of job opportunities. For workers during this period manufacturing employment was the principal means for getting connected with the expanding industrial urban economy. Through these jobs they were able to situate themselves in positions from which they could take advantage of improved opportunities and those still emerging. The common view shared by workers was that, if not they, at least their children and grandchildren would be the benefactors of their participation in the industrial manufacturing order. In other words, although industrial labor was highly exploitative (for example, workers worked long hours in very unsanitary and dangerous conditions for small wages), it offered them a ray of hope. Workers were socialized to be patient and obedient and to have faith in the culture of future progress. Molded by dreams of freedom and prosperity, these workers almost willfully became "sacrificial victims" for the next generation.

═ Moments of Friction within the Community

By the time Latinos came to make up over half of Suburbia's population in 1980 several major changes, which reduced vital resources, had become solidly entrenched in all segments of the larger society. The changes had started unfolding several decades before but really came into fruition in the 1970s. They transformed the social order and presented all citizens with new challenges for organizing their lives. The working class and the poor were affected most severely. These individuals and families, who historically have possessed limited amounts of resources, were left on their own to invent strategies they deemed appropriate for managing new social circumstances.

Economic Change

Perhaps the change that had the greatest effects on the lives of workers involved the economy. Since the end of World War II the new economic order of the so-called original industrial urban centers, or "central cities"—Chicago, New York, Pittsburgh, Philadelphia, Cleveland, and Detroit, which had all been established one hundred years earlier—was characterized by a shift in employment toward service occupations and the collection, storage, and dissemination of information rather than the production of tangible goods. Manufacturing and industrial work, which until around the 1960s had served as the backbone of the U.S. economy, were relegated to a position of secondary importance in these cities. Goods production began giving way to other industries, including clerical work, banking, legal services, insurance, merchandise retailing, health care, education, custodial work, hotel and restaurant work, security, and transportation.

While service occupations increasingly were becoming the new mode of labor participation in America's older industrial urban centers, manufacturing work was being relocated to suburban areas or small rural towns, the Sunbelt region, and in some cases to countries in the Third World. Several explanations have been offered for this outward transfer, or decentralization, of manufacturing plants. One focuses primarily on the influence of a series of innovations in transportation, communication, and production technologies. According to William J. Wilson,

Improvements in transportation and communication . . . made the use of open and relatively inexpensive tracts of land outside central cities more feasible not only for manufacturing, wholesaling, and retailing but also for residential development. . . . Concurrent with the growing cost and limited availability of land, tax rates rose, traffic congestion increased, and vandalism and other crimes that multiplied the operating costs of city industries mounted; many firms, previously restricted to the central-city locations near ports, freight terminals, and passenger facilities, began to rely more heavily on truck transportation and to locate in outlying sites near interchanges, the expanding metropolitan expressway system, and new housing construction. Moreover, the use of the automobile . . . freed firms from the necessity of location near mass transportation facilities in order to attract a labor force. (1980, 9)

The growing organization and militancy of the urban working class served as another leading condition that inspired owners of manufacturing firms to transfer their industrial facilities and operations out of the central city. Already by the turn of the century workers had begun forming labor unions through which they could collectively demand and secure better working conditions, higher wages, and health and related benefits. For the next fifty years this activity escalated fiercely, challenging the prerogatives of business owners and threatening their profits. The increasing centralization of the industrial labor force, triggered by the industrial city's need to have its workers living near their places of employment so they could walk to work, had backfired. Centralization enabled workers to maintain constant interaction and communication with one another, offering them the opportunity to share common labor experiences and grievances. In effect, it gave rise to the establishment of powerful working-class organizations, which began winning battles with the factory owners. Employers had great difficulty suppressing and overcoming these moments of worker resistance, and so they adopted an obvious solution: move.

Movement outward by manufacturing plants and operations began at the beginning of the century but was slowed down by the depression in the 1930s and the outbreak of the war in the 1940s. Relocation was resumed following the end of the war. In all instances the move was motivated by employers' search for stability, predictability, and security. That is, employers moved their plants and operations to locations where they were confident about maximizing their control over the process of production and minimizing workers' resistance to that domination. As indicated previously, the suburbs and small towns, the American South and Southwest, and sometimes countries in the Third World became the sites for the reestablishment of new factory districts. Owners of factories counted on finding a relatively powerless, nonunionized, and cheap labor force in these areas. They were aware that these new workers were automatically more isolated than those in the central city and that, as a result, contact with workers in other factories, with whom they might organize to protest against common issues such as adverse labor conditions, was to be much less frequent. Thus, relocation of industrial plants to areas outside of the central city came to represent the course owners relied on to secure a relatively passive and inexpensive assembly of workers. With this move owners of factories and other manufacturing industries could pursue their economic interests more efficiently.

A Shifting Population

Coinciding with the relocation of manufacturing plants outside of central cities were two complementary shifts in population, which greatly aided the restructuring of these cities and their neighborhoods. The first was the flight to the suburbs by white families who could afford to move. Daniel R. Fusfield and Timothy Bates point out that the general movement of people to suburban areas has been "highly selective": "It has disproportionately been young, employed, and white populations of central cities that have resettled in suburban peripheries, leaving the old, unemployed, and black inhabitants behind" (1984, 93). The second shift involved the massive arrival of African Americans, Latinos, and other poor ethnic populations to these "abandoned" cities. These various groups had migrated to cities in search of semiskilled and unskilled job opportunities in the manufacturing sector. It is safe to suggest that African Americans, Latinos, and other poor populations arrived in Chicago and other central cities possessing the same manufacturing skills as preceding groups of newcomers. During this same time, however, manufacturing jobs were being transferred outside of central cities. Further, the white population of these cities, who in the past had contributed to the operation of the city government, was on the move too, taking with it a large amount of tax money.

During the ten-year period between 1970 and 1980 the white population of the city of Chicago declined by almost seven hundred thousand. By 1980 57 percent of Chicago's total population consisted of minority residents, and there are predictions that this figure could increase by 10 percent more in the early part of the next century. In Suburbia, which had been experiencing a steady decline in population since the 1930s (for example, between 1950 and 1960 twenty-two thousand people left the community), the number of residents in 1980 was less than eighty-five thousand, less than 75 percent of the peak figure of a half century earlier. Construction of a major highway in the early 1960s, positioned along the north boundary of the community, contributed to the population decline, along with the general "white flight" noted above.

Despite this sharp population decline, Suburbia remained a fairly stable community. Of the city's seventy-seven community areas only three were more numerous than Suburbia in 1980. The fact that this community has not lost population as rapidly as the total city is attributable to the massive influx of Latino individuals and families. Latinos from other areas of the city as well as new immigrants poured into Suburbia during the 1970s, as indicated previously. Latino people did not become confined to specific sections of Suburbia; they settled throughout the different areas of the community. Latinos came to represent the majority of the residents in nineteen of the community's twenty-nine census tracts by 1980; in two census tracts they constituted over 70 percent of the residents and over 60 percent in seven tracts.

Toward a Service Economy

It was within this context of industrial relocation and population shift that the service economy came to flourish in the United States' central cities. It became very clear to city planners and government officials that the future economic health of these cities would be increasingly tied to their roles within the new service economy. In some cities the service economy was established around administrative headquarters and advanced services such as finance, insurance, and professional services. The growth of the service sector in other cities was fueled by burgeoning government and nonprofit service industries. Still others experienced a more diversified growth in services, with wholesale and retail trade making a substantial contribution.

By the late 1950s city planners in Chicago had already concluded that the city's economy would emphasize specialized methods of production, distribution, and marketing (City of Chicago, Department of City Planning 1958). A joint report by the business community of the city and Richard J. Daley, the newly elected mayor, showed that, since manufacturing would continue to gravitate to outlying, previously vacant land in suburbs and other areas, Chicago's future rested on a predominantly service-based economy. Particular emphasis was placed on improving the strengths of the central business district (CBD), which was located downtown, or in what is called the Loop. The CBD was expected to be the growth sector of the city's economy. All means of access to the Loop were to be improved, and the city was to do everything possible to encourage further office space construction to maintain and accentuate Chicago's position as a regional financial and administrative headquarters.

When it first originated the service economy was viewed with great enthusiasm and hope. It was thought of as a stabilizing force in the U.S. economy. Early optimistic forecasts, essentially rooted in an idea of progress which had dominated Western thought for over a century, emphasized a generalized upgrading of work and improved standards of living as manifested in the growth of managerial, professional, and technical occupations. Original projections speculated that "the U.S. [was becoming] the international center for highly skilled work and workers in finance, management and professional services, and information, leaving the 'dirty work' of manufacturing to less developed nations" (Hicklin and Wintermute 1989, 1). In addition, the favorable prognosis originally given to service occupations was viewed as stemming directly from the nature of services themselves. This idea stresses that, while goods-producing industries are sensitive to economic change, service industries tend to fluctuate less than others in terms of employment, wages, and production. In other words, when times are difficult economically people continue using the same automobiles, stoves, cameras, and other goods which they purchased years before. In contrast, although they may cut down on some service purchases such as travel and dining out, most people continue to use essentially the same level of services in periods of economic stress as in more prosperous times.

But not all city residents have achieved the benefits antici-pated from a shift toward a service economy. For racial and eth-nic minorities—who, along with poor whites, women, and youth have traditionally experienced severe labor market hardships—the coming of service occupations has inflicted a great deal of suffering. At best, these various groups have been locked into low-paid positions with little opportunity for advancement.

Problems of a Service Economy

One major problem facing racial and ethnic minorities, women, and young people in today's economy springs from the loss of hundreds of thousands of manufacturing jobs in central cities. Although there has been substantial growth in the number of jobs in service industries, it has not compensated for the decline in employment in manufacturing and other predominantly goods-producing, blue-collar industries, which once constituted the economic backbone of these cities and served as the spring-board for opportunities among the working class. Whereas in-dustrial jobs made up one-third of all jobs in 1920 at the national level, today that figure has dropped to one-sixth. In the case of Chicago, the city suffered a sharp decline of more than three hundred thousand manufacturing jobs between 1948 and 1977. The most pronounced employment losses occurred after 1967—the period during which racial minorities were becoming the largest portion of the city's population. In effect, the decentrali-zation of manufacturing industries and employment has left these various groups without traditional means for getting a foot-hold in the urban economy.

It is not surprising that labor force participation among ra-cial and ethnic minority workers declined sharply during this period of economic restructuring. For example, while the unem-ployment rate in Suburbia in 1960 stood at 3.6 percent, by 1980 it had already tripled to 9.4 percent. In two census tracts in which Latinos represented the majority of the population the rate of unemployment exceeded 20 percent; in one other it was more than 15 percent. A community's poverty level is another indicator of the effects economic restructuring has had on its residents. The official estimate of the percentage of people living under the poverty level in Suburbia in 1970 was 10 percent; by 1980 it had escalated to 18.7 percent. And in virtually every census tract where Puerto Ricans comprised the majority of the community's population, or the largest percentage of Latinos, the poverty level was higher than for everyone else. There were two cases in which the rate of poverty reached almost 30 percent.

Another problem accompanying the change from a manufacturing to a service economy is that service industries tend to have high concentrations of unskilled, unsheltered jobs with low wage rates. Between 1970 and 1985 more than thirty million jobs were created in service industries. According to Stanley D. Eitzen and Maxine Baca Zinn, however, "most were 'bad jobs' in the sense that they involved few skills, were poorly paid, had little responsibility attached to them, and provided poor job security. They have been typically filled by teenagers, women, racial minorities, and the poorly educated" (1989, 6–7). These low-level service jobs have not only eliminated the relatively secure, high-paid factory production jobs but also health and retirement benefits.

An additional problem associated with the shift from manufacturing to service is that, in responding to the overall city restructuring, pro-growth coalitions of downtown businesspeople, planners, newspaper editors, construction unions, real estate interests, and others decided to engage in efforts to retain the remaining white middle class and possibly attract some who had already left. These various groups believed that Chicago could not remain economically (and, for that matter, socially) viable if it became overwhelmingly populated by African-American, Latino, and otherwise poor surplus labor. The planners argued that Chicago would not be able to rejuvenate its economy without a strong and stable professional class, which, after all, represented the leading component of the service economy's work force. On this basis most of the policies recommended by the coalition, designed to improve the social and economic conditions of the city, significantly and disproportionally benefited the white middle-class population which had remained in the city. Suburban whites, who commuted daily to their jobs in the Loop, also benefited.

Benefits from employment in service occupations have not been realized equally by all workers for yet another important reason. Participation in the more permanent, high-salaried occupations of this new economic order calls for individuals to have attained high levels of education and/or training—mastery that minority residents have not developed because of the historic denial of educational equality. The significant role played by education and training within the service sector is explicitly described by Charles Hicklin and Wendy Wintermute:

Service industry occupations generally fall into one of three levels based on their educational requirements and earning potential. At the top level are those occupations that require at least a college education. These offer the higher wages and the most security and include managers and professionals. The middle level consists of occupations that may require some college and offer middle level wages. Included in this level are some sales and marketing occupations and upper-level clerical workers (e.g., office managers and executive secretaries). At the bottom are those occupations which require, at most, a high school degree. These occupations offer very low wages and little opportunity for advancement. They include service occupations such as janitors, security guards, and personal service workers, sales jobs such as cashiers, and clerical jobs such as typists, general clerks, and messengers. (1989, ii–iii)

Reliance on the system of public education—which establishes the academic foundation on which individuals pursue and attain the kinds of educational credentials necessary for securing the "good jobs" of the service economy—has disappointed many residents of Chicago. Described several years ago by William J. Bennett, then secretary of education, as the "worst education system of the nation," the Chicago public school system has been ineffective in servicing its poor and racial and ethnic minority students. As the *Chicago Tribune* indicated in a recent report on one elementary school studied by staff members during a period of six months,

The report from Goudy Elementary School classrooms, which are representative of the system, was stark and poignant. Such schools . . . are hardly more than daytime warehouses for inferior students, taught by disillusioned and inadequate teachers, presided over by a bloated, leaderless bureaucracy, and constantly undercut by a selfish, single-minded teachers' union that has somehow captured and intimidated the political power structure of both city and state governments. The outlook for improvement is not hopeful . . . mainly because public school students in Chicago are increasingly the children of the poor, the black and the Hispanic—a constituency without a champion in the corridors of executive and legislative power. To many politicians, public school systems such as Chicago's are a symbol of urban decay beyond help, a bottomless pit of incompetence, and a waste of both tax dollars and political capital. (1988, x–xi)

Latino youngsters from Suburbia, who in the majority of the cases attend one of two high schools designated to serve the community's school district, have encountered problems closely resembling those noted in the *Tribune*. Official rates for those leaving early from these two schools do not indicate problems. Conversations with individuals from the board of education's Dropout Unit, however, reveal contrasting results. In the words of one former staff member with whom I have spoken on several occasions, "the board covers up the real figures. Everybody in Chicago knows that. At [one school], the dropout rate is at least 40 percent. It all has to do with the students that they decide to count. When I was working there, my reports always showed different numbers. But these were not the figures that went into the official reports."

All the members of the Diamonds I came in contact with reported having dropped out of school. Several youngsters were suspended from school during their elementary years, though they were allowed to return. At the high school level one youngster was dropped during his senior year after school officials finally discovered that he had accumulated only four academic credits in almost four years. Most of the other youngsters had left school by their second year. Some felt that there was very little the high school could offer them. For others motivation to leave stemmed from the gang situation in these schools, as opposition gangs' control of the school environment made it virtually impossible for them to attend classes. Several others were coming to school essentially because of the drug-dealing operations they had established there; they stopped, however, when a law was passed in 1986 carrying heavy penalties for individuals caught dealing drugs in or near school buildings. With the enactment of this law youngsters recognized the minor significance that school played in their lives—that is, school buildings or playgrounds could no longer be used for generating monetary gains.

Given their negative experiences in the Chicago public school system, it is not surprising to find out that participation of Latino workers in the various service industries in the city has occurred in low-level occupations—food services, mechanics and repair, clerical and cleaning and building services. Latino workers are underrepresented in the professional and managerial categories, including legal services, engineering, business, insurance, and real estate. In the manufacturing sector Latino workers continue to be employed in declining industries. According to the 1980 census, the ten leading industries employing the largest number of Latino workers in Chicago are: furniture, lumber and wood products; other nondurable goods; nonspecified manufacturing; paper and allied products; miscellaneous manufacturing; fabricated metals; primary metals; motor vehicles and equipment; apparel and other finished textiles; and electrical machinery.

For a large number of Suburbia's workers manufacturing work represents the main avenue for earning a living. Of the 34,383 persons counted as employed in 1980, 42.7 percent were working in the manufacturing sector. In those census tracts where Latinos represent the overwhelming majority of the population employment in manufacturing industries is higher than for the whole community. And of the city's seventy-seven community areas only two others had a larger proportion of workers employed in manufacturing. One was Division Street.

The 1980 census also shows that, out of a total of 32,976 workers of age sixteen and over in Suburbia, one-third spent thirty to forty minutes commuting to work. For another one-sixth the distance to work took forty-five to sixty minutes. This condition suggests that most of the manufacturing jobs held by Suburbia's workers are located in areas outside the community. In addition, for many this condition creates a series of restrictions for securing work opportunities or remaining employed over long periods of time. That is, work trip origins and destinations increasingly reduce the chances of poor workers for finding permanent employment. Brian J. Berry and his colleagues indicate that resistance to commuting patterns on the part of these groups "is due partly to their lower rates of car ownership and to their lower earnings. Only half of Chicago area's black households and two-thirds of Spanish households own cars, compared to four-fifths of white workers. Black and Spanish workers earn on the average only two-thirds as much as white workers. The more people earn, the more time and money they are willing to spend commuting" (1976, 32).

For service workers from Suburbia only a small percentage are found in top-level occupations. In 1980, 38.3 percent of the community's labor force were involved in white-collar jobs. Only seven other communities in the entire city had such a small number of workers in these types of occupations.

Members of the Diamonds indicated that their parents work in service and manufacturing occupations. Most of those working in the service sector are employed in low-level jobs. An exception involves one family in which the mother is the principal of an elementary school and the father is an attorney; these parents are divorced. In another case the mother works as a registered nurse in a hospital located in the Division Street area. In another household the father is employed as a hairdresser in a local barber shop. In yet another case the father works at the airport driving a food delivery truck. Two of the mothers are hairdressers.

In terms of manufacturing employment several parents work in factories located outside Suburbia. Some of these establishments are situated in other city communities, while others are in suburban areas. One father is employed in a western suburb factory, a drive of over sixty minutes each way. Several parents worked in factories that had closed and moved elsewhere.

Finally, there was only one mention of a welfare family, which included an unmarried older son and a divorced daughter and child living in the same household. At the time of my research the son was working as a cab driver and the daughter as a switchboard operator for a downtown company.

Clearly, racial and ethnic minority workers, poor whites, women, and youth do not agree with business and civic leaders that the service sector of the U.S. economy represents a vehicle for their emancipation and empowerment. Rather, they tend to perceive the service economy as a curse whose cost in lost factory jobs is heavy, inflicting great pain as underemployment and poverty come to stand at the center of their everyday realities. In most cases service industries offer these groups low-wage, unstable employment. In effect, the shift from manufacturing to services has resulted in the creation of, in the words of Hicklin and Wintermute, a "two-tier society, by providing a small number of highly skilled and high paying jobs and a much larger number of low-skilled, low-paying, part-time and unstable jobs, with no apparent internal career ladders permitting upward mobility. The 'middle,' comprised of the sort of well-paid unskilled and semi-skilled jobs formerly provided by unionized manufacturing plants, was disappearing, along with middle-class incomes, middle-class lifestyles" (1989, 1).

Group Resistance

Latino residents of Suburbia have not accepted the degree of instability and insecurity which has resulted from their marginal participation in the service economy. They have resisted, escaped, or sought ways to change the crushing weight of the existing social order. As the majority population of the community,

Latinos have taken a very active role in developing a good part of Suburbia into a "Latino ethnic neighborhood," wherein some long-standing community institutions and structures have been changed and, in other cases, new ones have been created to provide the kinds of services that could help with the empowerment of Latino people. In other words, Latino residents in Suburbia have come to realize that they represent a critical mass in need of and which could benefit from initiatives tailored to their distinctive ethnic needs and experiences. As a result, Suburbia has come to represent one of the most recent hotbeds of Latino organizational activity in the city.

In recognition of the leading role played by the accumulation of educational credentials in the service economy and schools' historic neglect of Puerto Rican and other Latino children, several community initiatives were created to promote and improve the academic levels of Suburbia's students. One of the first was developed by Aspira, Inc., of Illinois, a community-based organization officially incorporated in 1969 to help with the building of youth leadership in the Puerto Rican community. (The word *aspira* means "to aspire," and students who participate in the program and activities of the organization are referred to as "Aspirantes.") Preparing students for college has always been Aspira's cornerstone. The organization functions around a belief that competent and productive community leaders must possess special skills and insights that only a college education can provide. Aspira seeks to identify and work with what it categorizes as "educable Latino youth." These youngsters are assisted through a multifaceted program of counseling, guidance, tutoring, and high school clubs. During the period of participation in these and similar programs and activities Aspirantes are instructed by staff members, particularly club organizers and counselors, in the history of their culture. It is expected that students' personal and professional lives can be meaningfully enhanced by a better understanding of themselves and their community.

Throughout the 1980s Aspira's central office was located in Suburbia, enabling youngsters from the community to have access to its various services and programs. One measure of Aspira's success is the number of community leaders who were early members of the organization. Former and present members are quick to point out, some with a great deal of exaggeration, that a large majority of these leaders are former Aspirantes.

As an associate member of the Network for Youth Services

(NYS), a coalition of Latino organizations that banded together primarily to promote collaborative work and to use their broad range of resources to more efficiently service Latino youth, Aspira worked with several related organizations to create a school program for a number of Suburbia's youngsters who had dropped out of school. Simply named the NYS Alternative High School, the program was started in the mid-1980s as a state-accredited academic institution. The NYS Alternative High School program revolves around a high school curriculum, offered primarily to Latino and Latina students (the overwhelming majority of whom are Puerto Rican), ranging in age from sixteen to twenty-one years old. According to school officials, most of the male students are former gang members (though it is commonly accepted that most are still active participants in different gangs), while the majority of the female students are teenage mothers. The NYS Alternative High School is designed to serve sixty students by a faculty of five to six teachers, a counselor, and a principal. There are no formal procedures for recruiting students; most learn about the school through word of mouth. Getting accepted into the program is quite difficult, primarily because there is an endless waiting list of students wanting to enroll. Clearly, this points to the fact that the problem in this community's conventional schools has reached its boiling point.

The massive school problems facing Latino students in Suburbia sparked the creation of another alternative high school program by the local Boys and Girls Club. Originally established in 1948 as a branch of the Boys and Girls Clubs of Chicago to serve the youth and families of Suburbia, for the last ten years the club's directorship has been in the hands of two second-generation Puerto Rican young men. Both have given the various programs and activities of the club more of an academic orientation. They both endorse the idea that the club's programs must be geared toward improving the academic backgrounds and needs of Latino youngsters. They also hope to sustain the academic interests of these young people through other programs and activities that are not considered academic.

In the early 1980s the Boys and Girls Club put into place its alternative high school program. The school program serves the very same type of student as the NYS Alternative High School. One major difference is that the Boys and Girls Club's program enrolls forty students instead of sixty. Another major difference is that the Boys and Girls Club's program is built essentially around one teacher, who is responsible for teaching most of the subjects in the curriculum and coordinating participation by teachers from the students' traditional home schools. Additionally, student placement is made principally by the students' regular high school counselor.

This procedure of commissioning the alternative high school program with the responsibility of serving as a "dropout center" for those students unable to make it through the regular school program can be viewed as a way of relieving schools of students they do not know how to handle. And, though the present director of the club might admit to serving the schools in this way, in a conversation I had with him he was quick to elaborate: "I would take these kids at any time, even if the schools feel that they can't handle them. I don't mind being a drop-off center. At least, these guys have somewhere to go. The real challenge is working with them. We want to change their habits, to make them become interested in education. That's what we want to do. And that is the bottom line."

Another major area for which a great deal of community-based organizational work has been devoted in Suburbia during this period of structural transformation is housing. The leading efforts have been undertaken by the Hispanic Housing Development Corporation, established in 1975 to ensure that the city's Latino populations and communities be awarded their proportional shares of public housing funds, which were estimated in the 1970s to have been near 1 percent. The specific purpose of the Hispanic Housing Development Corporation, according to one of its own reports, "is to develop and manage affordable, quality housing for low to moderate income families and elderly within Chicago's Latino communities. Hispanic Housing also seeks to expand employment and training opportunities for Latinos in the fields of real estate development, property management, construction, and marketing" (1989, 1).

The first housing development project of Hispanic Housing consisted of the rehabilitation of a 160-unit housing complex in Suburbia. The total cost of the project was estimated at over six million dollars, and it was completed in 1980. Two years later the organization fulfilled its second project in Suburbia. It refurbished a housing structure of 196 apartments at a cost of over twelve million dollars. All rents were subsidized by the federal government. In all, the Hispanic Housing Development Corporation has been responsible for fifty million dollars worth of housing development in Latino communities throughout the city. Of this, over 50 percent has gone into projects in Suburbia.

In terms of employment opportunities and work development skills in the area of real estate, in 1983 the Hispanic Housing Development Corporation created a property management division to oversee the operation of its various housing development projects. The management entity is primarily responsible for the maintenance of the development corporation's properties. Since its inception the management unit has been self-sufficient. It has generated property management fees from tenants and has used these gains to finance its administrative and operating costs and to administer its properties with greater fiscal control. To date, the property management division is responsible for a total of 557 units located in twenty-seven separate buildings.

Following the commercial lead of earlier ethnic groups in Suburbia, some Latinos in the community responded to the combination of changing economic conditions and population shifts by entering business ownership. Two original neighborhood streets, which in the past had represented the shopping centers of the area, were joined by another directly south to constitute the commercial heart of the community. Lining these streets is a wide variety of Latino stores and shops, demonstrating openly that a good part of Suburbia's commercial district is now dominated by the Latino culture. Puerto Rican, Mexican-American, and Cuban food stores, restaurants, and jewelry stores have come to represent some of the leading business establishments in Suburbia. Many of the advertisements, posters, and billboards found throughout the community are in Spanish or bilingual. Neon signs announce the goods and services offered in this commercial district. Restaurants advertise *comidas criollas* (authentic indigenous cuisine). Grocery stores specialize in tropical fruits such as mangoes, plantains, coconuts, guava and tamarinds; and vegetables such as *batatas* (white sweet potatoes), yuccas, yautias, and yams. *Puerto Rico, Mexico,* and *Cuba* are often part of a business's title, as in the bank name El Banco Popular de Puerto Rico. Flags of these countries are prominently displayed in shop windows. During local election years posters for Latino candidates are also found on many windows. Wall murals in the district depict other aspects of Latino culture.

The rapid growth of the Latino population in Suburbia during the 1970s created a so-called Latino market, and Latino entrepreneurs in Suburbia emerged within the ethnic experience itself. Indeed, it became clear that the Latino ethnic community possessed a special set of needs and preferences that could be best served, and perhaps could only be served, by those who share those needs and know them intimately, namely, the members of the Latino community itself. Possessing the ability to furnish Latino cultural products and services, Latino entrepreneurs were quick to find a niche within the ethnic community. The important point about this business activity is that it involves a direct connection with the ethnic group's homeland, or culture, and knowledge of its tastes and buying preferences—qualities unlikely to be shared by larger, non-Latino competitors.

Latinos have had special problems caused by the strains of settlement and adjustment to the larger society, which are aggravated by their distance from conventional institutionalized mechanisms of service delivery. Consequently, the business of specializing in the problem of adjustment and participation in the larger society became an early avenue to economic activity. Latino-owned travel agencies, law firms, realtors, and accountants became common in Suburbia's commercial environment. Such businesses frequently perform myriad functions far beyond simply providing, for example, legal aid or travel information and reservations.

To a large extent trust is an important component of one's use of a service, and the need for trust pulls the newcomer who is Latino toward a business owned by a Latino. Persons who share the same background generally become the clients for these enterprises. In addition, Latino people prefer personal relationships over reliance on impersonal, formal procedures. Such predispositions further increase the clientele of those businesses specializing in adjustment problems.

One major consequence of the Latino business concentration in Suburbia is of particular importance: the promotion of ethnic identity through cultural dominance of the area. That is, the size of the Latino ethnic market now provides a scope for specialists whose services would otherwise not be in sufficient demand. Customer traffic strengthens the group's dominance of the community, which, in turn, leads to high visibility of goods and services with a strong Latino component. Thus, the Latino ethnic market becomes an attractive place for Latino shoppers for the goods and services it provides. It is also significant for the role it plays in maintaining ethnic identity.

For another group of Latino residents in Suburbia the informal economy has come to represent a practical response to its members marginal status within the service sector. By informal economy, I mean unregulated income-generating activities or activities that avoid state requlations. Some activities prevailing in

Suburbia's informal economy, also evident in other communities, include numbers selling (*la bolita*), street peddling, and homework (for example, babysitting, food preparation and sales, sewing, and jewelry and cosmetics sales). Many of the individuals engaged in informal economic activities are poor. These are individuals who are in desperate need of obtaining the means of subsistence for his or her family. For them conditions of low wages and lack of benefits in the formal sector have sparked them to turn to informal economic activities. There are also individuals engaged in other informal work, though they are employed in the formal sector as well and should not be considered as poor (for example, individuals who moonlight as plumbers, electricians, car repairmen, or secretaries in the evenings or on weekends).

In effect, informal economic processes cut across the whole social structure. Both the poor and members of technical/mechanical professions are active participants. It is not surprising to discover that some of these individuals generate incomes higher than those of workers in the formal economy.

But it is gang-sponsored drug dealing that stands out as the most widespread and visible informal business establishment operating throughout Suburbia. Along with the Diamonds, it is believed that there are nearly a dozen gangs and/or sections of the same gang carrying out drug-dealing operations in the community. Gangs have divided Suburbia into various open markets, each controlled by a different group. There are times when a single gang might hold absolute dominance over several turfs. Drug dealing can be found on most street blocks, corners, and schoolyards of Suburbia.

And of course, increased alarm over the spread of drug dealing and its relationship to crime rates in Suburbia and other areas in the city has led to the formation of a large number of government and local neighborhood initiatives geared to eliminating this type of informal economic enterprising. Taking cues from the federal government's "War on Drugs" legislation, policymakers from the state of Illinois and the city of Chicago have publicly adopted a belligerent attitude toward individuals involved in drug use and dealing, particularly gang members. Since the early 1970s every plan has been fashioned around one central idea: to severely punish apprehended and convicted dealers. All of the legislation, policies, and programs have been aimed at removing so-called drug criminals from society by imposing large mandatory prison sentences. In addition, these "criminal drug laws" have been enforced relentlessly without regard to possible appeals due to technicalities, such as those relating to legal and human rights, or to ideas about avoiding giving youngsters criminal records whenever possible.

Several special antidrug and antigang enforcement units and programs have been developed in Chicago to fight the so-called drug war at the grass roots level. Various efforts have targeted communities like Suburbia which have developed reputations as major areas of drug distribution, marketing, and use. Both the ideological thinking and financial support with which the programs have been put into effect embody the vision of the federal, state, and city governments in terms of how to best deal with these "enemies of the state." The ultimate goal has been (and still is) to put apprehended dealers behind bars for a very long time.

One initiative was the formation of an undercover police force called the Metropolitan Enforcement Groups (MEG), whose members come from existing law enforcement agencies (including local police, sheriff's officers, and the Illinois Bureau of Investigation). MEG members wear plainclothes, drive sporty cars, and try blending into settings believed to be havens for drug dealing and use, such as high schools and colleges and universities. In their daily spying operations members of MEG are aided immensely by high technology gear consisting of videotape cameras, thirty-five-millimeter binocular cameras, and portable radios. Information is also secured through the employment of paid informants as well as through the practice of undercover drug buys. Again, all of this activity has been geared to enhancing the rate of arrest and conviction among users and dealers.

A narcotics conspiracy squad, involving the collaborative participation of the Chicago police department and the U.S. Attorney's Office, the U.S. Drug Enforcement Administration, and the Internal Revenue Service, was another major unit formed to fight street-level drug dealing in Chicago's neighborhoods. The major responsibility of the task force is to target "narcotics gangs" of five or more dealers operating on a daily basis. The plan calls for the apprehension and prosecution of dealers under the federal Continuing Criminal Enterprise statute, a measure that carries a minimum sentence of ten years and a maximum of life imprisonment.

Another action taken to curtail illegal drug activity called for the recruitment and training of racial and ethnic minority agents to move against African-American and Latino drug distribution centers in the city which had been virtually undetected because of cultural and language differences that could not be penetrated by white officers. According to city officials, since a substantial portion of major drug dealers in Chicago and the state had African-American, Mexican-American, and Puerto Rican backgrounds, the most effective way of handling this situation was to hire "their own kind," individuals who know the ins and outs of the particular culture and its people. Thus, in the same way that Latino agents came to represent some of the best weapons in the ongoing war against drug cartels in Latin America, racial and ethnic minority agents could be recruited and trained to infiltrate drug gangs in their own communities. It was expected that these culturally informed agents would more easily identify, apprehend, and arrest those people from the community who for a long time had been on the "wrong side of the law."

In the face of the inability of government and the police alone to combat the enormous power that drug dealers have wielded for so long, parent watch groups were organized and thrown into the drug war. These groups were made up of an army of angry neighborhood parents who mobilized themselves to go after the drug dealers who threatened the well-being of their children and had taken over the neighborhood. These parent groups refused to be held hostage in their own neighborhood. In effect, they had become convinced that their neighborhood would not be cleaned up until the residents, themselves, stood up and took charge. And that is what they did and are still doing.

To stop drug dealers in their tracks parent groups have employed a series of interrelated tactics. They have given major emphasis to identifying and then harassing drug dealers, followed by the submission of reports to law enforcement agencies, which in turn, move to capture the dealers.

In Suburbia and Division Street representatives of over twenty community-based groups joined together in the early 1980s and formed a council to spearhead the organization of neighborhood residents to combat drug dealing and use and associated gang violence. The council embarked upon a massive campaign of letter writing, publication of newspaper articles, reports, and ads, and participation on radio and television programs to convince parents about the need to become involved in cracking down on drug dealers and users. The thrust of these various efforts was to help with the establishment of formal parent groups and neighborhood block patrols which would then become responsible for watching neighbors' homes, telephoning neighbors to keep them informed of crimes in the community, showing up in court to support victims, and pressuring police to enforce curfews for youth. WE CALL POLICE and BLOCK WATCH stickers were displayed on windows and doors of houses and buildings throughout the area.

It is difficult to determine the outcomes of these various initiatives. One thing is sure, however; city police officers, neighborhood parents, and other adults are now pitted against gang members and those youngsters believed to be drug users and pushers. It has become a war between "good" and "evil." Gang members, dealers, and users of drugs represent evil.

That some parents are encouraged to side against neighborhood youngsters, some of whom are their own children, suggests society's lack of understanding about the everyday experiences of these youngsters and how best to deal with them. When parents agree to take action against these youngsters they confirm the views shared by members of the Diamonds pertaining to adults' unwillingness to listen to and take seriously their descriptions and interpretations of the things they experience. The mobilization of parents has resulted from information the authorities have provided about gang members. After being around these young people I learned that they wish to be working with parents and other adults rather than against them.

The lives of members of the Diamonds evolved within a context of an impotent public school system, scarce economic opportunities, and a drug war that involved the participation of nearly every adult as part of a system of neighborhood surveillance. These youngsters are aware of what they are up against. As Elf explained it, "Nobody cares. We don't have a chance. We're fighting against other gangs. We're fighting against the police, and against our teachers and even our own people from the neighborhood. They are all after us."

In addition to understanding how conditions in their immediate social surroundings have affected their lives, members of the Diamonds recognize other, more external circumstances that impact them the same way. Although not always discernible, decisions and actions taken outside their neighborhood trickle down to shape their life courses on a given day, week, month, and year—and for many years after that. One example is captured in the following exchange in which Tito talks about how he was officially maintained in his high school's enrollment records for almost four years, although he was chronically absent from his classes the entire time:

Felix: You indicated earlier that you dropped out of high school. How long were you in school?

Tito: I was there until my senior year.

Felix: Why would anyone drop out of school during the senior year?

Tito: They kicked me out.

Felix: What happened?

Tito: We got a new principal, and he found out that I had accumulated four credits in four years, so he decided that he had to get rid of me.

Felix: Now, how is it possible for someone to accumulate four credits in four years? How did you do that?

Tito: After my freshman year I hardly came to school. Sometimes I would come to my homeroom and then leave. I would walk out of the school and go and hang out with my friends and with the girls. And, although I was hardly in school, they kept passing me. So, by the time I became a senior I had four credits, and that's when the new principal came in.

Felix: You mentioned coming to school and going to your homeroom and then leaving the school building. Why did you even bother going to this class?

Tito: Well, this was not a class. This is where they take attendance. This is where they check to see if you're in school. And, see, if you're in your homeroom, they mark you present for the whole day. I heard that the reason they did this was because the money the government gives the different schools has to do with the number of students who are in the particular school at a particular time. So, it was important for the school to keep me; this way they would not lose money. Schools are just like everybody; they just want to make money. So, you know, it's a law—well, not a law but, you know, something like a regulation that said that if a school has so many students it got more money.

Felix: I see. You also mentioned that this changed when a new principal came in.

Tito: Well, I don't know if it changed, but, at least in my case, I was kicked out.

Felix: And why do you think that this happened?

Tito: For a couple of reasons, I think. There's a new law that said that attendance was going to be counted in every room, and the new principal did not want to get in trouble. So, they finally called my mother and told her that they had dropped me from school.

Felix: You said there were two reasons. What is the other?

Tito: Oh, yes. Well, this guy was Latino. He's not there anymore. But, anyway, because he was Latino the community was expecting a lot from him, like miracles. They wanted the school to educate people and they believed that the principal was responsible for making this change. You know, this was the time when the community and parents got really involved in school and began putting the pressures real hard. So, this guy started cleaning house, and I was one of the rotten apples that he got rid of.

Flaco's deep displeasure over the government's unwillingness and meager efforts to facilitate employment opportunities for youth like himself is indicative of his awareness of how external conditions affect his life. His indignation was publicly revealed in the spring of 1990 when I invited him, Tito, and Danny to speak on their gang experiences to my students from a social problems class. In a seemingly angry response to a student's query about his desire, or lack of, to secure conventional work Flaco said, "You know, I want to work, but they are cheap. You know, the government doesn't want to create jobs for us. Instead of doing this, they take the money for themselves. They are greedy. They're just businessmen. They only care about themselves. And, you know what, if they don't do something around here soon, there is going to be more problems. I remember some of the older guys from the neighborhood when they were my age, and they used to get summer jobs, and they could count on those jobs. They knew that when summer was here they were going to get a job. Today there are no summer jobs around here. To get a summer job you have to go to another neighborhood, and then there will be thousands of other guys applying for a few jobs. It's the government. They are cheap. They're going to have to get off their mighty horse and start sharing."

In speaking to the issue of the international drug trade, Coco indicated his knowledge of how his behavior is directly inspired by elements external to his immediate environment, particularly the way it manages to locate its retailing component in poor neighborhoods such as the one where he lives. He also pointed out the reasons the larger society seems to be doing so little to prevent it: "I don't know, but to me it seems like a setup. We work selling drugs, but have you ever stopped to wonder why it's people like, you know, people like Latinos, Puerto Rican people, and black people that are selling drugs? I know that these drugs come from places far away from here. We don't grow this shit here. Maybe we should so we can keep all of the profit. You know, maybe all the money could belong to us. Have you thought about how the smokes and the cane get into the country, into our community, into the community of black people? You know, the government talks about the guards who patrol the borders and shit like that. And on television, yeah, you see people talking about how the government made a large bust. And they say that's because of those guards on the borders. That's all bullshit. They are letting all the shipments of drugs come in because it's all political. People are making huge amounts of cash. But, then, we are the ones that pay. We can't get jobs, but we can certainly get our hands on as much reefer and cocaine that we want."

That Suburbia is central to the lives of members of the Diamonds is without question. That these young people have developed an understanding for the wide-ranging universe of oc- currences taking place in the larger society and neighborhood and how these have exceptional consequences on their lives is also without question. Members of the Diamonds have come to recognize all the forces around which they must organize their lives. These young people know a great deal more than what we want to give them credit for. They know a great deal about them- selves; they know what their world is about. They also know how little the conventional world has to offer them. It is within this context of social awareness and understanding that their gang involvement becomes comprehensible. In what follows we will discover the courageous ways in which these young men have fought over time against the many powerful forces that have con- fronted them.

Chapter
3

Turning: Becoming a Gang Member

"When I turned I took a lot of stuff, a lot of blows. I was hit from head to toe, but, still, it was real bad. Some guys hit me on my chest, while others hit me on my stomach lots of times. They all wanted to see how tough I really was. They wanted to know if I was good material for their gang. You have to show that you have heart, that you are not afraid of taking a beating. There are times when a guy develops a reputation of being tough and a good fighter. In these cases the gang is pretty lenient. But in the majority of the times the gang makes sure that they do not accept guys who, instead of fighting and protecting the gang, prefer running. They don't want that—cowards are not allowed. So, the test comes when you turn. They hit you all over the place. In my case, as I told you, I showed that I could take it. I didn't drop, but I was hurting for a week."

"I only told this to my closest friend—well, he saw me, anyway— but I got a rib broken when I turned. I was hit by a crowd of guys. There were about twenty guys, and they all took blows at me. And some of those blows landed on my ribs. The doctor called it a rupture, something like that. I was real skinny at that time, so a lot of things used to hurt me. But I managed. I never told the guys how I felt, they thought that, like everybody else, I was going to be hurting for a while."

These two accounts vividly characterize one of the most horrifying rituals making up the culture of the youth gang: the violation, or, as the youngsters put it, simply the "V." The violation ceremony involves the dispensing of physical violence through fist blows, leg kicks, and other such acts to members during three distinctive encounters. One involves the initiation rite. The second use of the violation occurs during times when a youngster decides to resign from the gang. Third, it is employed to discipline youngsters whose behavior is in violation of particular gang rules.

During the V ritual, administered during meetings of a gang section or those involving the various sections that comprise the larger gang organization, would-be violated members must walk singularly through the middle of a long line made up of other gang members. While walking the violation line the penalized gang member must endure the assaults furnished by those standing on either side. (The size of the line ranges from ten to fifty individuals, depending on the type of meeting being conducted.) The young man is permitted to protect himself from the onslaught, but, just as important, he must also keep from falling to the ground; otherwise, he must start the walk again from the beginning of the line. If the youngster falls and refuses to repeat the walk during an initiation rite (called the "V-in"), he is not allowed to become an official member of the gang. He can agree to repeat the walk at that very same moment or at a later time. The latter practice is most often followed, though there are cases when youngsters simply forgo turning. If the ceremony is held for the purpose of "getting the V-out" (that is, the official resignation of a member from the gang), a refusal to begin the walk again after a fall entails having to remain an official gang member.

Without a doubt, the V-out ceremony is mostly aimed at administering a great deal of severe physical punishment. There are two moments when the V-out penalty is ruthlessly carried out. The first involves cases in which a youngster is perceived as having acquired a great deal of information and knowledge about the Diamonds' operation. Anxious fears are expressed toward such a member because it is believed that he could serve as an "intelligence agent," passing on his accumulated knowledge of the gang's operation and activities to opposition gangs or to police officers. Punishment given to this member is extremely relentless, for it must guarantee the maintainence of his loyalty to the Diamonds, even though he is no longer an official member. Elf made this point clear one day when the gang was planning a meeting to V-out a member who had been with the Diamonds for over five years. I had come by early that afternoon—it was around 3:00 P.M.—and noticed seven members walking away from the turf, though each was going alone and in a different direction. I called Elf, and he signaled for me to join him. I ran and caught up with him. He told me that they were trying to round up as many members as possible because there was going to be a V-out ceremony. He said, "Have you met Polaco? Yeah, I show him to you one day. He is the one that looks like a white boy; he is white and has blue eyes. Well, Polaco got locked up for a couple of years. He got out and came back and did some time with us out on the streets. He knows a lot of shit, man! He knows about some of our boys who are inside the joint. He knows everything we do because, since he did time, the chief started to trust him more. He was given more respect. The chief put him real close to him. And he learned a lot. But now he wants to walk. And we got to show him that what he knows is only for him. We don't want him telling people what we do and where and shit like that. So we got to get as many of the guys to be here for our next meeting next Friday. That's when we're going to do it. And we want to do it to him real good."

The other instance in which the V-out ceremony is carried out most remarkably involves members who have "been nothing but trouble for the gang." For these young men the turbulence of the violation act is believed to be well deserved on the grounds that they have been troublemakers, not good and committed "team players." Coco captures this side of the V-out ceremony in discussing the day he plans to walk. "When I get ready to quit, I'm going without being scared. I know what awaits me. I have seen it so many times before. And I also have dished it out myself. But in my case things are going to be cool because I've been pretty cool with everybody. I'm not going to be afraid. And you know why? Well, let me tell you. You see, I respect people, but, you know, when people mess with me, well, then I got to mess with them. Here you got to protect yourself because, if you don't, then everybody is going to take you for a sucker, you know, for a sissy, you know, a punk that can't protect himself and shit like that. So I can give it. But I'm cool with my partners. You know, my mother has always had this saying, she would always say, even to this day, she tells me this saying in Spanish: "*El que la hace hoy, mañana lo paga"* (Those who do it today, tomorrow will pay for it). And that's how it works in our gang. If you fuck up now, if you decide to be a prick all of your life, you know, messing with others, using other people, trying to take other people's money, or stealing from them, boy, that's it. When you try to leave, everybody crowds on you. When one of these kinds of guys decides to get his V-out we make sure to call the meeting at a time and place so everybody can come. That's really nasty. We try hitting him everywhere. Because the fucker deserves it."

On the other hand, violations carried out for the reparation of an infraction committed by a member tend to be less harsh. It could be a case wherein only the chief, or mainhead, of the section performs the discipline. Even on these occasions, however, failure to walk the line successfully after being hit means having to repeat the act at another time. These youngsters wind up up receiving a double penalty. Rafael describes one of the last violation ceremonies he witnessed, involving a member who had committed an infraction of a fundamental Diamond rule. "We were having this meeting last Friday. The chief was talking about not fucking up. He was saying that he needed people to be cool because he heard that the police were planning all kinds of raids against us. And that they were going to come after us on Fridays. He thought that it was going to happen this weekend. So, he be telling us this stuff, then, all of the sudden, he started shouting. He started shouting at Manny, this dude who is a dealer. He's no big deal. He doesn't have people working for him. He works the streets for his main man, that's about it. But the chief said that Manny was trying to work other streets on his own. The cat was getting greedy; he didn't want to work together with us because he wanted all the customers for himself. So, instead of working with us in our hood and our turf, he went to this other street, away from our hood, and he tried doing his thing. And that's what fucked him up because one of our boys saw him. So, the chief walked over to Manny, and then he ordered two guys to violate the shit out of him. They hit Manny upside his head, all over his chest and shit. The dude was hurting. He was holding his stomach; you know, that shit hurts. Then the chief told him to get the fuck out of his face and to start following the rules of the organization. Then he told everybody to remember what can happen to them if they decide to fuck up like Manny—that the rules of the organization are supposed to keep us protected and that the reason we sometimes get into trouble is because people violate the rules."

In more general terms the violation ritual serves as a mechanism of social control, used principally for keeping gang members "in their places" while simultaneously serving to reinforce the social order or arrangement of the organization. Through the act youngsters get a vivid picture of the plausible consequences that will result from the refusal to follow gang-specified rules. Additionally, this mental image operates as a stern warning for those thinking of discontinuing their partnership and/or gang-determined relations with the Diamonds. From their initial violation encounter (V-in) to direct participation in subsequent ceremonies involving new members or those who have violated certain rules, youngsters witness or experience firsthand the treatment they are likely to undergo if they fail to comply with principles of individual and social behavior as established by the gang. Gang members come to experience the various hazardous conditions and accompanying forms of punishment existing within the structure of the gang; indeed, part of their purpose is preventing gang members from plummeting into one of these "V-circumstances." Clearly, the violation ritual is an important way of establishing and affirming the power and control by the gang over its individual members.

Of the three V rites of passage, I will focus on the V-in, for it most poignantly demonstrates the kind of physical torture these young people are willing to suffer in order to "turn," that is, to become official members of the gang. Youngsters' willingness to undergo and endure this vicious physical onslaught suggests the high appraisal they give to the organization. The agonizing course these youngsters are determined to cross also points to the limited opportunities they believe to exist in the larger society. Members of the Diamonds have come to accept the idea that, since society cannot offer them the means with which they can make something positive of their lives, the physical punishment of the gang's violation ritual is not too big a price to pay. They have taken physical punishment before—it comes with living in the inner city—so, why not take more, particularly when it can open doors that have shut to them during an entire lifetime?

Although these young people agree to the physical punishment embodied in the V-in ceremony, it is important to regard it as the culmination of a process through which their attitudes and views have been shaped. Like those of us who make the decision to gain practical experience about a social phenomenon before developing an opinion on the most appropriate course of action to follow, members of the Diamonds, whether consciously or not, proceed along the same lines concerning the V-in. This behavior was built up over time through contact with situations and individuals, which combined to condition their perceptions of the gang as a social organization capable of satisfying some of their basic needs and/or serving as a shield against conditions of injustice and suffering. In effect, when youngsters develop a perception of the gang as an instrument of empowerment which can transform their lives in an affirmative way they make the decision at last to walk the V-in line and to become official members of the gang.

What forces and conditions are responsible for shaping this perception and subsequent behavior? Or, to put it simply, how did these young people arrive at the point where they would willingly undergo the V-in violation to become gang members? The stories provided by members of the Diamonds and my various observations of them indicate several factors and conditions, stemming primarily from neighborhood and school environments as well as police treatment, that motivate youngsters to join the gang.

═ *Neighborhood Influences*

The youth gang made up a good part of the social and physical landscape of Suburbia during the preteen and adolescent years of the members of the Diamonds. Although it is a fact that Suburbia possesses and displays many middle-class characteristics, for nearly two decades this neighborhood has served as the home base for a large number of youth gangs. It is believed by most youngsters that the number of gangs and/or gang sections is still growing as attempts to create new drug-dealing turfs continue in earnest. My conversations with members of the Diamonds, however, revealed ambiguous accounts of the history of their gang. Oral history accounts—those stories passed down from one generation to the next for the purpose of preserving and reinforcing, in this case, the history of the gang and maintaining its authenticity and identity—are hardly uniform. Similarly, they know just as little about other gangs. In most cases, however, some of the youngsters might recall the names of members who were really "down for the gang" (the most committed members) and some of the "courageous" sacrifices they carried out to save the gang from oblivion, though they are not capable of providing a thorough description of the particular actions taken. Many different and, at times, contrasting renditions of intergang fights represent the episodes most commonly described, and in these stories, of course, the Diamonds always emerge victorious.

One thing the youngsters are all certain about is that a large number of youth gangs were present in their neighborhood when they were growing up. Youngsters were unable to recall a day when the gang was not part of the neighborhood, as evidenced in the following exchange in which Coco speaks about living alongside several youngsters who were gang members.

Felix: Which gang members do you remember when you were a kid?

Coco: Oh, by my house—there was Jimmy and Francisco. They were cousins who lived in the same building. Not in my building, but they lived in the same building. That was next door to me.

Felix: Were there other gang members in your neighborhood?

Coco: At this time, of course. On my block there were several others. But, you see, gang members don't hang out on their block because they don't want their parents to know that they are bangers [members of a gang].

Felix: So, where did you see the other gang members?

Coco: Different corners, but mainly on the schoolyard. That was always their favorite place for hanging out. It still is.

For Flaco the gang represented a natural fixture of his neighborhood—an everpresent element of the physical and social environment. In an almost poetic way he stated, "Like the apartment buildings, the sidewalks, and trees of the neighborhood, we [the gangs] were all part of the same thing. You can't get the gangs out, they were there when I was a kid, and now we are here for the new kids. As a matter of fact, I don't think anyone can remember a day when there were no gangs in the city. A lot of people blame us for gangbanging, but there were gangbangers a hundred years ago. What do you think the Mafia was? That was a gang just like some of the ones in the neighborhood. They were really organized and had a lot of money, but, I tell you, some gangs today are developing that way. Maybe we will be one."

Indeed, the short-lived histories of members of the Diamonds have unfolded within a social environment wherein the youth gang has persistently played a central role. Thus, young people from the neighborhood have grown up witnessing and learning specific elements of gang culture. These youngsters have been altogether familiar with the workings of the gang for a very long time; at least, they have known about the more visible ingredients of the organization's cultural milieu.

Lobo's experience with the local neighborhood gang is a case in point. He grew up on a street block where several youngsters affiliated with a gang were his friends, from whom he witnessed what he defined as "the nuts and bolts of the gang." He recalls, in particular, the tightly knit relationships present among gang members and how those affiliations served as the major force for establishing and maintaining cohesiveness within the organization. When asked to elaborate on this idea Lobo responded: "The fact that those guys got along so well, that's what told me about how things worked with the gang. They cared for each other. They were brothers; the blood was the same. To me that's really what made the organization. People are always putting down gangs because they say we're punks and up to no good, but they don't understand what gangs are all about. I remember seeing these guys; hey, they cared about each other more than a lot of other people who are not in gangs do. That's what I remember the most about the guys from the hood; they were always looking out for each other. And that's exactly what we did when we became gang members. I had several friends that I was really close with. They were like my brothers. We did everything together."

In the case of Tito, growing up among the local youth gang meant witnessing various fights and hearing the different explanations offered by gang members to justify their behavior. Tito recalled being in seventh grade when he first learned about gangbanging: "I didn't really know the meaning of gangbanging until one day on the schoolyard when I saw this fight. After the fight there were two guys who were cursing each other and talking bad about each other's gang." He added; "After the fight in the schoolyard I learned that these guys didn't like each other, and the way to settle their differences was through throwing down. Then they began saying things like, 'This is my hood. If I see you here again, I'm going to kick the shit out of you.' So, to me the fights were started because some guy was in some neighborhood where he did not belong. I kind of thought that it made a lot of sense because I wouldn't want people from other places coming to my neighborhood and claiming it for themselves. My mother had told me stories about how Puerto Rican people used to live in different neighborhoods, like over there where you teach now at DePaul, and how other people came and took over their neighborhood. I thought, and still do, that we have to make claim to what is ours. We want our neighborhood for us, so we have to protect it. So, when I was in grade school, I saw these guys doing things that I thought were necessary to do, like protecting their section of the neighborhood from other gangs. And, you know what, ask any of these guys around here what they think about their neighborhood, they all going to tell you that that is the most important thing for them. So, learn to care for the neighborhood—that's really important. I learned this lesson a long time. Not that I was making plans to join a gang in those days, but it's crazy that it would happen to me."

Youngsters learned to accept the neighborhood as something that was very personal, for its identity and character were believed to originate directly from all of its residents. Just as important, as Tito indicated, was having learned that maintaining neighborhood social harmony was an essential responsibility of gang members; any disturbance might make public a youngster's gang affiliation and identity as well as the drug-dealing business. Youngsters could hardly afford to reveal their covers since it might jeopardize their business routine and invite local parental involvement, which could, at the very least, lead to public embarrassment and humiliation. This point is well described by Coco: "The guys in the neighborhood never fought there, on the street. I learned something that I found was true when I turned, and that is that you take your business to the alley or to the schoolyard or even to someone's hood, but you don't do it in your own neighborhood. That's a sign of disrespect. Besides, you don't want people in your neighborhood to know you belong to a gang. They begin harrassing you and stuff. Even to this day my mother doesn't believe that I'm a gangbanger. I have gotten locked up a couple of times, but, since this happened in other turfs, I always told her that I was jumped by punks from opposition gangs."

He continues: "The first time I was locked up it happened in the hood of the opposition, so I had to call her to get me out. I told her that the cops fingered me because I looked like someone they were looking for. The police told her that I was a banger, but she believed me instead. And I kept telling her that they were lying and stuff like that. But, you see, if I was around the hood doing stupid shit and people saw me and told her, then she be like, 'La Sra. [Mrs.] Maria told me this about you,' and I couldn't deny it because Puerto Ricans believe a lot in what their neighbors tell them."

Association with neighborhood peers (nongang members)

also served to fill out members of the Diamonds's mental images of gang culture. In most cases, friendship groups, sports teams, clubs, party groups, and other cliques were already long established, and, like other youngsters, members of the Diamonds joined these groups for companionship, social enjoyment, and recreation. And when a group member was acquainted with someone affiliated with the gang he would facilitate interaction and communication between the rest of the group and the gang. The role of this young man was to legitimize each group, for each was suspicious of the other. He would vouch for his neighborhood friends, endorsing them as trustworthy to his friends in the gang. On the other hand, his depiction of the gang was aimed at cultivating a clear and convincing picture with which his friends could evaluate the gang as an authentic and positive youth organization. Rafael describes the way he first made contact with members from his neighborhood gang: "I don't think I was really afraid of the gang. But, as you know, when you're a kid a lot of things scare you. You have your parents telling you all the time not to hang out with this group or that other group. Your older brothers and sisters tell you the same thing. But my friend knew some of the guys, and because of him I started hanging out with the guys. And because of him I was treated just like him. I was OK to them."

Elf experienced a similar process of gaining familiarity with the gang, as he indicates in the following dialogue:

Felix: When was the first time you came in contact with the gang?

Elf: I was young. Maybe eleven.

Felix: How did this happen?

Elf: Through my friends. Several homeys of mine who were connected brought us in. It was really no big deal.

Felix: Why not?

Elf: Well, I used to think that what those guys always wanted to do was to beat the shit out of you just for the fuck of it— something like wilding (doing crazy things)—you know, that they would beat up people because they didn't have anything else to do. And that they picked on guys like me because we were small and weak, and, you know, we were what you call helpless. You know, we couldn't defend ourselves. That's how I used to picture it.

Felix: So, what did you find out?

Elf: They were not like that. They talked to you. I was too young, so they were not interested in me as a member. They didn't mess with me. They treated me alright. At first I was surprised because they were cool with me, and I did not think that that was the way I was supposed to be treated. But they did, and I'm glad.

Felix: What did you do with them?

Elf: Well, not much. Whenever I saw them or they saw me I would say, "What's up?" If I was in the hood and they were hanging out, sometimes they called me over. We would say, "What's up?" But it was something loose, but I became uptight with them and they with me.

A contrasting experience affecting the peer group also served to heighten youngsters' mental image of gang culture. There were many times when the peer group became the target of harassment from different neighborhood gangs because of the former group's determination to maintain a "neutron" status— that is, having no affiliation to any one gang. Though they lived in the same neighborhood, some youngsters chose to remain unaffiliated with the geographically immediate local gang and those from other neighborhoods (that is, they were "hanging in the middle"); as a result, their status of neutrality was constantly being tested by various competing gangs. Punishment inflicted on these youngsters, then, was not aimed at coercing them to "turn"; rather, it was meant to ensure that they would remember the importance of remaining neutrons. There is a constant fear on the part of gang members that neutrons might decide to become informants for another gang or, worse yet, be coerced into providing law enforcement agents with news and information of activities being carried out by some gangs. Even as neutrons, these youngsters learned the importance of loyalty within the gang's scheme of things. They witnessed the gang's activities and perceived the gang as an association committed to maintaining confidentiality among its members as well as by people in the neighborhood. As one young man expressed it, "Back when I was a neutron, I learned that with the gang it's the secret that counts. You got to be tight-lipped about what's going on. So, now I understand that it's important that you don't tell people anything you know about the gang. Even talking to someone like you is dangerous, except that they know you, so that's OK. In a way that's how things should be. I really like that. We don't want neutrons to be rats, to be telling people about our affairs. Another thing that we don't want is people in the neighborhood to be calling the cops on us. That's not cool. We don't let people get away with that shit, boy. If they give us this respect, then we give them the same thing. But, if they don't, then we are going to be on two different sides. We like the neutrons and other people to be on the same side with us."

It is important to add that trying to maintain a neutral status is no small task for youngsters growing up in Latino neighborhoods today. To grow up in an area controlled by one gang or, worse yet, by several gangs means having to identify oneself with at least the spatially nearest group. So Latino youngsters learn very quickly to adopt a series of protective or defensive schemes; in particular, they learn the cultural symbols of the nearby local gang as well as those of the various competing others in order to masterfully use this knowledge in appropriate situations. In this way they will not be accused of choosing sides or displaying more loyalty to a given group than to another. Tito recalls being in this plight:

Felix: What's the meaning of "represent"?
Tito: To know what gang they're from and what gang they dislike and know who's hood you're in.
Felix: So, what happens when you represent?
Tito: You throw up their signals. That tells them that you're straight. That you respect them.
Felix: When did you start learning about these things?
Tito: I was going to the seventh grade. That's when I started learning a lot about gangs and what they were really about.
Felix: What did you learn?
Tito: Their symbols and the signs and what they mean and what's for the gangs. They write their symbols up, to tell people which are their symbols, and where they are at, and things like that. If the symbols are upside down that means another gang defaced the gang's wall. I learned that when that happens that's a sign of disrespect.
Felix: And which gangs were around your neighborhood?
Tito: They were opposites. There were Folks and People where I lived. They were all around, so I got to know all of them— where to hang out and where not to hang out.
Felix: So, you had to learn to be a neutron?
Tito: Right, and, if I did choose to be with the opposition, which one would be best for me? Like, if I lived in one territory, I should be more or less on their territory than on the other side. Because, if I had to spend most of my time there, I

would have to be on their side. It depended on where I was at and where I would go.

Through these various neighborhood experiences, all of which occured before their teen years, members of the Diamonds were able to accumulate a fairly extensive body of conceptual information as well as practical knowledge with which to form opinions about the functioning of gangs. Overall, their emerging views toward the gang were being shaped in a positive light. For them there was nothing necessarily immoral or inappropriate about being a gang member; in fact, they defined gang members as "straight," "cool," and "together"—people to be admired and not resented. Contrary to public opinion, which tends to prescribe a criminal label to gangs and their members, ever since their adolescent years youngsters belonging to the Diamonds, like Elf, have pictured the gang favorably.

Felix: You told me you knew things about the gang when you were in eighth grade. What exactly were your thoughts of the gang at that time?

Elf: It was cool—a bunch of guys who cared for each other and who were having a good time.

Felix: And that's what *cool* meant to you then?

Elf: Yeah, it said that you were part of a bunch of guys who trusted each other. The gang was cool in that way. There are some guys who don't know how to act cool. They are always showing off. They be trying to impress you. They think that's cool. But it's not. They be lying and telling stories about their homeys. In the gang you can't do that. In the gang you don't carry on that way because the rest of the guys are going to think that you are a big jerk. You ain't a nobody because nobody cares for you.

Felix: Are you saying that other youngsters were not cool because they did not belong to the gang?

Elf: I guess they could be cool, but, you see, the gang forces you to always be cool, together. You know, this is your homey, and brother, so take care of him, don't rat on him. That's what makes the whole thing cool, like a family. Everybody is a friend and brother. You treat people like a brother, like family.

In the same way Tito developed an affirmative and supportive impression of the gang. He still recalls early times when those who were known to belong to a gang were granted a great deal of fame: "I went to a school where there were all kinds of nice girls—you know, a bunch of really attractive Puerto Ricans and Latinas—and they were always checking us out. And, since I have always liked girls, I used to check them out, too. And the girls in school used to think that these guys [gang members] . . . everyone in school used to think that these guys were cool, and they were because they had all the girls and stuff. I thought that they were bad [meaning "good"]. They talked kind of bad, you know; they had their own kind of way of expressing themselves. They used to walk bad. They had this hip walk, and everybody knew that they were in gangs. And the clothes. Well, you know, everything about those guys was really together. Hey, I began wondering how it would be to be in a gang. These guys seemed to be having a good time all the time. Not that I went and joined the gang right there and then. I was still too young, I guess. I guess I was still scared. But I used to think in a good way about bangers at that time."

Benjy offers a similar characterization of the gang, perceiving it as the most rational organization for youth participation: "The gang seemed to control the things I wanted. I was kind of a dork when I was in elementary school. I was really into my studies, and I didn't get involved in any stuff that the gang was doing. But then I began to see that they had the girls, that people listened to them, and stuff like that. I never expected to become one of them, but at that time they were something to be admired. They were popular. You know, this is where it's at: That was my initial attitude of them. And, even though my parents and older brothers were always telling me to stay away from those guys, I kind of admired what they stood for and the way people used to like them."

▬ *School Environment*

In addition to these neighborhood influences and motivations, a wide range of school-related experiences contributed immensely to the youngsters' positive outlook toward the gang, which in turn, led to their subsequent affiliation with it. Their affirmative judgment of the gang and decision to join were developed over time as contact and interaction with teachers and some schoolmates already familiar with or actually belonging to gangs resulted in their being labeled "deviants" and troublemakers and treated accordingly. Members of the Diamonds responded to these conditions by joining with others so labeled and engaging in corresponding behavior. In response to teachers' labelling them negatively, which in most cases occurred during their elementary school years, youngsters adopted different forms of "oppositional behavior" (for example, misbehaving in the classroom, refusing to do work in the classroom and at home, fighting with classmates, and cutting school). Additionally, some of the labeled adolescents began associating as an informal group, developing a distinctive subculture within which they could examine and interpret what was going on in their lives and in school as well as determining the most appropriate set of activities for dealing with these conditions. Thus, beginning at the elementary school level, the oppositional, or resistance, behavior carried out by these youngsters in response to their being labeled was akin to gang activity. What was happening to these young people was that, unknowingly, they were undergoing early preparation for a later stage in their teenage years (during high school) when they would finally join the gang. Against the actions of high school classmates who were involved in gangs and who tended to consider them members of an opposition gang, Flaco, Coco, Elf, Lobo, and the others sought protection by turning. Since primary grade and high school years produced different experiences of nonconformist behavior, I will consider the two periods separately—the former first.

The Elementary School Experience

Some members of the Diamonds recall that as early as the fourth, fifth, and sixth grades some of their teachers were already ascribing the label of deviant to their activities. In turn, many of these youngsters sought out others similarly labeled for comfort and affiliation. Whether for misconduct or alleged academic deficiency, or both, some of the youngsters remember being publicly branded as deviant by their teachers. They responded by adopting the popular stereotype assigned to anyone bearing the label, and their classmates and other school peers treated them accordingly.

Even at the time that I met these youngsters it was difficult for many of them to talk about their days in elementary school. This experience was associated with much pain as teachers and staff refused to understand and respect their cultural and socioeconomic class background. In the case of Flaco, on several occasions he started mentioning how unfairly he had been treated, only to break sharply and stop talking altogether or dicuss something totally unrelated. One day it finally happened: He carried the description of that "awful experience" to "the end." It was a day I was spending with him and Benjy. Benjy began to tell me about his wife and child, his future plans, how confused he was, and how much assistance he could use to figure out how to accomplish some of the things he wants to do. He then asked me about how I managed to survive life in *el barrio*. How did I make it? I told him about my high school experiences. Afterward Benjy asked me to drop him off at a friend's house on the north side.

I then stopped at a Burger King with Flaco for some food for our way back. Flaco asked me again to talk about my high school experiences. I had already shared this part of my life with Flaco. Perhaps the first time it had not carried the significance that apparently developed during this second round. In any event, I repeated my difficulties with U.S. schools, especially having had to accept a grade demotion because I was not fluent in the English language when I transferred from a school in Puerto Rico to one in Chicago. I told him that I had been an excellent student in Puerto Rico, but in the Chicago school system teachers did not involve me in the goings-on of the classroom because they assumed that my language difference was obviously a sign of some sort of academic deficiency. I sounded angry when I told Flaco how I felt attending a school system that had defined me as defective because I spoke a language different from the one used formally there. My tone took on a sour quality when I told him how upset I had felt to be physically present in the classroom but with my teachers refusing to see me. I also told him how I was able to survive. Being a baseball player and participating on the school's baseball team was a means through which I gained self-respect.

It was at this point in our relationship, about five months since our initial contact, that Flaco opened up and began talking freely about his life as an elementary school student. I had shared information with Flaco about my personal life which he probably did not expect was even there. Apparently, he felt compelled to reciprocate and spoke openly to me.

Felix: On several occasions you have mentioned having failed the fourth grade. For what reasons?

Flaco: That's when I started grouping around with the boys.

Felix: How old were you?

Flaco: I was about ten, maybe nine. It was like my second fourth grade, though.

Felix: And what do you mean by hanging out with the boys?

Flaco: Well, the boys, we started groups, right? And there be groups where the guys you think you want to hang out with, you be classifying them, like, these guys, they cool, or these guys are nerds or act like dorks, or these guys are too smart for us and teacher's pets, and then other guys were alright. And, then, we'll judge each other, we'll be coming to school at a certain time and meeting each other there, and then we try to get seats next to each other and to talk to each other and stuff like that.

Felix: And which one of the groups did you belong to?

Flaco: I was with the bad ones—the ruthless.

Felix: Where does that classification come from?

Flaco: Well, 'cause that's how the teachers would put it in our heads, you know, and "You guys are the troublemakers," and "You guys are too loud" and "You're too this, and you just don't want to listen, and you just want to sit in your chairs and lay there."

Felix: Why were you placed in the group you called the bad ones?

Flaco: I don't really know. I guess I used to be hyper. I was always moving. It was no problem . . . it was no problem with other people. But in school the stuff was boring, and I would tell the teacher about it, so she kept saying no and to be quiet and shit like that. So, because I talked back and didn't want to sit still she started treating me like if I was retarded or like shit.

Felix: What happened after you were grouped into the bad ones?

Flaco: We started hating the other kids. The classification did not stop here because from there my fourth grade teacher would know the teacher you were going to next, so she already says, "Keep an eye out for these kids because these are the troublemakers," and stuff like that. And we would think, "Well, why bother because we're in the bad group already?" And then we'd say, "You see all the other kids in our class, too, but they're the smarter ones, or they're the dorks, this and that." And they just call us the troublemakers.

Coco's school experiences in his fifth grade are almost identical to Flaco's. In his opinion his teachers and other school personnel refused to recognize and accept his excessively active behavior as part of his normal personality. Instead, it was misinterpreted as a sign of mental instablility. As a result, he was summoned to take a series of diagnostic tests and later placed in a program for the learning disabled, to which he responded by displaying the kind of behavior prescribed in the label or anticipated by school personnel. He says, "I was put into a class for slow learners, you know, students that the school thought were disturbed and had problems with reading and math. They also thought that I had mental problems. You know, they said that, because our mental problems, we didn't know how to work with numbers or that we couldn't read. What they were saying was that I was stupid and retarded—you know, that these kids can't do the work because there is something wrong with them, in their head. And shit like that."

"Anyway, that became my permanent class. . . . I was in a classroom where most of the students were Mexican and black and I was the only Puerto Rican, so they would pick on me and try busting me up. But one day one of my friends transferred to my classroom. They thought that he was retarded too, and the two of us began fighting with these other guys. We would fight, throw ourselves on the floor, and do crazy things like. And throughout all of this sometimes we would get caught, and sometimes we wouldn't. One day I really got caught, and the people there decided to give me tests to see if I was crazy. I told them that I wasn't crazy, that I behaved like that because that was what I wanted to do. But they gave me these tests, and they placed me in this classroom, and I was there until seventh grade. From there I transferred to [another school], and they put me in a classroom with the so-called bad-ass kids. I told them to put me out because the problem was going to continue since I acted that way because I wanted to and not because I was retarded or crazy."

"But, you see, people in school, like your teachers and principal, these people don't listen to you because they are supposed to be right all the time. They lied to my mother about the way I was acting. They convinced her that it was true that I was crazy. They told her that the best thing for me was to go into this classroom because there were going to be just a few of us and the teacher could work better with us. What we did was to fight all the time. But my mother, she knew how to speak English, but, you know, not that good. She is a Puerto Rican, and you know how that is. She didn't want to be disrespectful; she is always talking that talk. And then my father, he was working, so they didn't call him. She was tricked to sign that paper. She says it herself now. She knows that I'm hyper, but that's how I am."

In Lobo's earliest school memories one of his teachers' name-calling routines led to his subsequent stigmatization and treatment as a troublemaker. He described how, after being labeled a troublemaker for arriving late to class on several occasions, every mischievous act that happened in school was blamed on him. "One time," he says, "we were in the hallway, walking to the bathroom, and someone threw a rock through a window, and all the kids said, 'Lobo did it.' But since I was with everybody else in line they changed the story to 'one of Lobo's friends did it.' You know, I became the explanation for everything that went wrong in that school. So, I retaliated by fighting. And there were lots of fights."

"My first fight was with a guy for stupid little reasons. This was about the fourth grade. I threw him into the filing cabinet. It was a stupid reason because the teacher wanted us to go around . . . we were doing something with science and using test tubes, and then we had to collect them from each student. I collected them from one side, and he collected them from the other. We ended up running into each other in the middle, and I told him to leave them there and I'll bring them up to the front. He said, 'No, I'll do it.' So, I said fine, and I walked over to one of the small tables and put it on top there. I guess he was picking them up so fast that he hit the chair, and they all fell over. And then he blamed me for it. He told me that he thought I was going to take them all up to the front first and then let him come back and get the other stack. And I said no—I had figured he wanted to take them and left them right there for me to take up. Then he started yelling that it was my fault. I told him to fuck off. The teacher came and started yelling at the both of us, but primarily at me. And the minute she turned her back I slammed his ass into a filing cabinet where he had about five of his front teeth knocked out. Then I got suspended—like, big deal. Ever since then I had this attitude that, if you were going to mess with me, I was going to mess with you physically."

The stories of these and other youngsters serve as evidence of the difficulties of attending school while knowing that they were being viewed as the cause for every disruptive situation there. Always being blamed constituted part of the emotional attack these young people suffered so early in their school experiences. As the bearers of the troublemaker label, they remember being cut off from participation in activities involving other "normal" students, though they believe they possessed the academic skills and knowledge required for performing classroom work at the same level of proficiency as their peers. Lobo recalls never being called on by the teacher: "I was real good in science and math, but the teacher never bothered to let me work with the rest of the class. I was a troublemaker, and I was supposed to stay by myself. What was I supposed to do?" Not surprisingly, this treatment gave rise to a self-fulfilling prophecy whereby several mechanisms conspired to make Lobo, Coco, Flaco, and the others fit the image teachers and others had developed for them. As indicated earlier, all of these young men began drifting into oppositional behavior by joining other students and friends who had been treated as they had been. These youngsters began to recognize the common fate they shared with others like themselves. In Coco's own words, "If the teachers and everyone else thought that we were bad, we started to show that we were. So, we started doing a lot of bad things, like hitting some kids and even talking back to the teacher and laughing at her. In a way, it was kind of fun because here are these teachers thinking we were nuts and we would act nuts. That made them feel good. Like I told you before, I'm sure they felt like they were right. But for me that was an opportunity to act stupid, to act silly and like a clown. It was fun because some of the other students liked to see us act stupid. So we had like a crowd, a crowd that we wanted to give a good time."

For several other youngsters this oppositional behavior was undertaken to serve as a rationale for neutralizing the treatment they believed their teachers and peers were unfairly bestowing upon them. Rafael describes it in the following dialogue:

Felix: What was your "acting up" like?
Rafael: We were bad. We didn't listen. We used to fight all the time.
Felix: What were you hoping to get from acting up?
Rafael: Well, it was no big deal. It was my way of getting even. You know, teachers were saying and doing all this nasty shit, and I wasn't going to put up with that anymore.
Felix: So, what were you doing these things for?
Rafael: I guess I was trying to protect my dignity. There was nothing wrong with me, but they didn't believe me. To them I was like shit. Just because you're Puerto Rican or Latino, they treat you like dirt. I guess I was trying to protect myself.
Felix: And about your fights with your classmates, what were you trying to show?
Rafael: Well, we used to think that they were always kissing the teacher's ass because they were put down, too. They

thought that by being ass kissers they were going to be treated OK.

Felix: And why did you pick fights with them?

Rafael: We didn't like them. They were punks. And this was our way of saying "Hey, we're not afraid of the teachers or you." It made us feel good. We felt like we were in control. This was our way to feel powerful. You know, we didn't want to make people feel afraid, but we didn't have nothing to use to get at these people. So, like a lot of people do, like you see in the movies, the best weapon to use is force.

Clearly, resistance patterns of thinking and acting furnished these young people with reasons that appeared rational and sound for continuing to challenge the generalized view that they possessed undesirable traits allegedly associated with their culture and behavior. In other words, since the treatment given to these youngsters denied them the conventional means of carrying out the routines of everyday life in the classroom (including moral support), the youngsters, of necessity, developed an oppositional system of strategic activities.

For members of the Diamonds the disparaging treatment by teachers and peers dampened their interest in school and led them to conclude that it was far better to stay out of school than to be victimized by their teachers' constant verbal assault and sometimes physical punishment. These young people lost interest in school and stopped attending—or "cutting school," as this behavior is popularly referred to—as early as elementary school. They began experimenting with staying out of school, continued to do so on an occasional basis, and finally became regular "cutters." Tito explains his experience of despair and frustration with one of his teachers and how it influenced him to not bother taking school seriously: "Well, there was one lady, and I don't remember her name, I just remember that I was in fourth grade, and she was one of those ladies that liked to yell at the kids and call us names. She was always calling me names, like slow and someone who couldn't do work and stuff like that. And I didn't like that. I guess that's what lost my interest. And this teacher had a triangle ruler, and if she caught us talking she would hit us on the hand for it, and I'm just one of those people that hates to be hit like that—I don't know why. So, that's why I never like to get into the school too much. I never went to school. When I went I never did any work or homework. I was never really interested in school when I went there. So, even at that age I found ways not to come to school. There were times when I left for school but never got there because I would go someplace else and hang out with my friends."

What was really upsetting for these young men was the constant explicit and implicit disapproval, or put-down, of those things that were at the core of their lives. It was extremely difficult for them to know that their culture was being assigned a negative value or, at best, not given appropriate respect. Carmelo reflects on how one of his teachers was always ridiculing and belittling Puerto Rican children in her class, at times suggesting that they voluntarily accept becoming welfare recipients. He recalls losing his respect for this particular teacher. He also believes that this experience took away much of his interest in school.

Felix: How did you like [your school]?

Carmelo: I did not care for it. The teacher was a crap. I remember a few times she would say things like "We are supporting your parents who are on welfare and are living off of us." She said this several times.

Felix: What grade was this? What was your teacher like?

Carmelo: Fifth grade. I was a child. She was a white teacher who lived in Northbrook—you know, one of the wealthy suburbs along the lakeshore and far away from people like you and me. I remember she'd be talking about how her daughter had a closet full of clothes.

Felix: And what?

Carmelo: And she would talk about her daughter. One time she [the daughter] complained that she needed another blouse, and she [the teacher] went into the closet and counted something like sixty blouses, or something like that—some outrageous number. Imagine, this bitch had sixty blouses and was complaining. Why did she [the teacher] have to tell us that shit? We were poor. Imagine sitting there hearing this shit when you know how rough things are at your house. But that's how this lady was. And several times, again, she would say how her and people that worked with her or people that were like her were supporting people who were on welfare. And I was on welfare—I was on welfare for many years.

Felix: How did you feel after hearing your teacher say these things?

Carmelo: I used to bring good grades home. I was taught to stay shut. I used to talk a lot but never to adults. I did not want the word to get out to my parents and grandmother that I was being disrespectful. My grandmother was the last person I wanted to find out. She taught us manners the Puerto Rican way. You know, she lived with us for a very long time. When my mother and father were working she was the one that raised us. And she raised us the old Puerto Rican way. After my mother got sick, she [the grandmother] stayed living with us. I did not want her to get angry at me for doing bad in school. So I did not say or do anything when my teacher said those things.

Felix: How much did this bother you?

Carmelo: Obviously, it bothered me a whole lot because it still clicks in my mind. I still hear her saying that. When I left that class to go to another class I did not miss her at all.

Felix: What did you do to counter what your teacher was saying?

Carmelo: Well, as I told you earlier, I liked school a lot—even to this day. But I was little; I was a child at that time. So, I decided to forget about all this shit, so I would cut school as much as I could get way with. At that time we took most of our classes with the same teacher, so we couldn't simply cut one class. We had to cut the whole day. And I did. It was better not to attend school than to go to school. People tell you all the time to go to school—that without school you are nothing. Maybe that's true, but they never tell you about the kind of shit that you have to put up with in school. At that time I was not willing to put up with insults. I have changed very little over the years.

What was once a degrading and demeaning "in-school" experience became a pleasant, desired, and sought after "out-of-school" activity. Youngsters found pleasure in staying out of school, an experience that at first was very frightening.

Lobo: In the fifth grade I left for a semester. Almost half the year I missed out because I didn't want to go.

Felix: What happened?

Lobo: Just picking up trades from the streets. It just stole my attention away from school. So, as far as wanting to come to school, I'd leave early in the morning, making everybody think I was going to school, but I just hated school. After that I just stayed out.

Felix: So you were leaving home but not going to school?

Lobo: Right, that was all in the fifth grade. I just got really fed up. I figured leading a life of hanging out in the streets with my homeys on the corner or in a game room would sometimes be smoother than being in the classroom. These guys were better than classmates. These guys show you they care. They were better than anything that was inside those doors.

For these young people entering into associations with other labeled and/or mistreated peers signified their first unofficial connection with gang behavior. These youngsters were carrying out activities that closely resembled those of the gang, though they were not gang members. In addition, in several cases there were older youngsters already involved with the gang who made it possible for Lobo and Tito and the others to come into direct contact with the gang. Although these young people were not official members at this time, nonetheless they were provided with opportunities to witness for themselves several key activities being performed by the gang organization. And to these they responded affirmatively, developing an image of gang members as role models to be admired.

It is clear that these youngsters did not accept their elementary school experience as an anomaly or a transient social phenomenon. During their adolescent years the institution of education and its agents, the administrators and teachers, were already being experienced as antagonistic elements in their socialization rather than as facilitators of their goals.

The High School Experience

The above presentation indicates that during their elementary school years several members of the Diamonds had already participated in some of the activities of the gang, mainly hanging out, or "grouping," on the street block or schoolyard. Their involvement during this time, however, remained marginal and unofficial. For the most part turning occurred when youngsters began attending high school.

Tito was sixteen years old and in his second year of high school when he became an official member of the Diamonds. His decision to join the gang was heavily influenced by a friend of whom he thought very highly and with whom he had developed a tight bond. "I was about in my sophomore year or, like, the end of my freshman year," he recalls. "I had a friend who was in a gang and who was telling me about gangs and how things were, and, I don't know, just one day I went, and my friend was kind of bubbly because he had been drinking, and we went to his neighborhood, and I was talking to his chief and stuff, and, then, I just turned. When I joined, like, four or five other guys that were like my neighbors, right there by the crib, they turned too, and we all joined at one time. Since we were friends we all decided to join—because we used to hang with the gang, but we were neutrons, and we just decided that we might as well become something since we hung out on the corner and gangbang anyway, and so we just decided to go for it. We just did it just like that. We didn't think about it or think, "Wow, what is this?" We just slid into it. We knew what we had to go through to become official gang members, but we were willing to. We wanted to be part of the gang and be recognized like that."

That his friends played a major role in Tito's life can be witnessed from the way he talks and describes them. Tito always sounded exhilarated and proud, demonstrating a special enthusiasm for the relationship he and his friends have been able to maintain over the years. One such moment can be captured from his response to my prompt, "Tell me how how you turned together": "Like, there was a main seven of us in my neighborhood. We stuck together all the time. When we joined this gang we became real good friends, and we always shared with one another. Like, my friend would need a boom box, and I would have it at my crib; I would say, 'Here, take the box; you can use it.' Or, like, if the summer was real hot and I would have an extra fan, I would give it to my friend and say, 'Hey, here's a fan.' Then we would talk about it. I would say that I needed a T-shirt, and sometimes they would go get me a T-shirt, or stuff like that. It became more like brothers instead of friends. We became like real true brothers, and we treated each other so good that it made sometimes being out there all right. It made it, like, you're out there with people you know. It's not like somebody you never saw or you never met in your life. You know you finally joined, and you'll be with people that you really know and trust. It's alright; it's not what a lot of people think."

"And in my school there were other gangs that always thought of us as belonging to this other gang. And we always denied it because really we weren't. I mean, we would hang out, but we were not with them. One day one of our boys got smashed, and he was crippled really bad. So, we decided, if this is going to happen again, if the opposition is going to wait to catch us alone when there is no one around us, we might as well join. This way they know that messing with us is like messing with the whole organization. So, that was another reason that we finally hooked together."

Coco attributes his turning primarily to the influence one of his high school friends had on him. This friend was exceptionally regarded for he had served as one of Coco's sources of emotional support during elementary school. This particular friend had earned Coco's trust and confidence by sticking up for him at a time of need. So, when the friend recommended to Coco that he become a Diamond he replied affirmatively and with little hesitation. He recalls: "Well, my friend from [this other school] had caused so much spill there that he was given a transfer and was accepted at [my school]. He turned Diamonds, and it looked to me that he was having so much fun in the organization—like, 'Let's go and do this, or let's go and stump that punk or that other punk—and that's how I always wanted to be. I had taken so much shit from my teachers and principals—I always wanted to get on top of someone and slam him to the street top. So, I decided that I wanted to be a Diamond. From there on I attended the meetings. We started chasing hoodlums from the opposition. I was dope [having fun]."

Flaco also joined the Diamonds on the advice of some friends who had provided him with protection over time against other gangs. Flaco had grown up in a section of Suburbia which served as turf for several gangs, making it quite difficult for maintaining a neutron status. His friends helped him remain unaffiliated and sheltered; other gangs understood that to mess with Flaco could be considered an act of disrespect against the organization he was closest to. And, like in Tito's case, since he had spent so much time hanging out with a particular gang and had developed a close affinity with its members, deciding to become an official member seemed like the most natural and rational decision to make.

Felix: When did you join the Diamonds?
Flaco: Four and half years ago. I was a freshman in high school.
Felix: And what were the reasons for joining?
Flaco: Well, let me see. More or less the reason was because I was already hanging with them since I was small, so I was in the neighborhood. And I had a couple of real good buddies. And I had protection by them.
Felix: What exactly did your friends say to you?

Flaco: Not much. It wasn't like they were forcing me. They just told me to turn. It was no big deal.

Felix: And what did you do after this?

Flaco: I turned. I believed them. You know, I had to get my V-in; they told me about that. It wasn't like if I didn't know. It was tough, but we all had to go through that.

Felix: You mentioned earlier that your friends gave you protection. What's protection?

Flaco: Protection? I had backup. You have to have Folks on your side, 'cause, if you're not in one gang, you're not in another gang, and they always be asking if you got a sign, and if you're on this side, and you get rolled on anyway. And you have nobody on your side, so you're still gonna pick a favorite of your Folks or People. I don't know, kids could stay neutron, but it's very hard, and it's very rarely you see kids that are neutrons. And the ones that are neutrons—they still got a favorite; they like Folks better, or People. And the Folks or the People can't let you see them too much on the other side. Like, if you're a neutron, and you're in favor of Folks, if the Folks see you in People's neighborhoods, they're gonna think something about it. And then that's when you got problems.

Felix: So one of the reasons why you joined was for protection, for backup?

Flaco: Yeah. I liked chilling out with them, too.

Felix: What did you like about hanging out with them?

Flaco: Everything's fun. Sometimes we would ditch school or take a day off. We just go, we get a couple of cases of beer, we drink those, and then we'll go up to the top of the roofs and look over. Police come, and they chase us down. We just had a lot of fun, do a lot of kinds of things.

Rival gang labeling, as already suggested above, was another major reason for turning Diamond. It is a common practice for gang members in a high school to consider new, incoming students as belonging to the opposition. In doing so, when initial contact is made the new students are treated according to the views held about them.

Most confrontations tend to occur in schools where members from various rival groups are enrolled. Suburbia's school district is served by two high schools. According to members of the Diamonds, one is faced with with rival gangs from different neighborhoods primarily because the community has a major busing program that enables students from areas other than Suburbia to be accepted for enrollment. Some believe that the school is represented by twenty different gangs from several neighborhoods. Additionally, members of the Diamonds were attending this particular school during the period of ethnic population change; there were, thus, racial clashes with several white gangs as well. In effect, the school atmosphere was filled with gang tensions.

The other high school is the home of a single gang. Therefore, gang rivalry and gangbanging is less frequent than in the other school. Most of the Diamonds attended the former; they indicated having experienced an enormous amount of gang-related problems there.

In describing the reasons for joining the Diamonds, Elf recalls having been the target of one gang because some of its members believed he was with the opposition. He says, "I was a smart student. I would never let things get in my way, school-wise. But once I got into high school that's where it all dropped out of sight. 'Cause I used to live in one neighborhood, and I would go to another neighborhood, and they would never see me there, and they would say, 'What you be?' 'What gang are you in?' 'Where you live?' And I'd tell them were I lived, and they already assumed that I was one of them, when I wasn't. Or they assumed that I was with another gang when I wasn't that either. Then I decided, 'Man, if they're going to keep on rolling on [jumping] me, and I ain't got nobody to back me up, I better turn.' And I did."

Elf's response led me to probe further since I found it extremely difficult to identify or single out someone like him as a gang member with the same ease he had described. To me Latino youngsters from *el barrio* seem to look the same; they seem to dress, walk, and talk the same. So, I said to him, "Let me try to put this in some perspective. You're saying that, whether you are in a gang or not, once a gang identifies and labels you as a gang member, they start treating you like a gang member. Now explain to me, how is it that someone like you gets identified as a gang-banger?" Reaching back to touch the ponytail he was styling and then bringing his hand up to his left ear to touch his earring, Elf explained: "At one time it used to be colors, but that's out. People don't wear colors anymore; that's too obvious of an identification. Colors are no good for the business. But it's usually the way a Latino looks or the way he expresses himself, the way he brings himself to people. Let's say, when you first saw me, what'd I look like to you? A little hoodlum, right? But you can't say that, but the way I look, usually the hair, the way I have my hair, the way I style my hair. It's things like that that make me look like a gang-banger. I don't know, but there's a certain thing to a person, what he does, the way he walks. It's the way you bring yourself to people."

Rival gangs labeling was the major reason Gustavo decided to turn. Gustavo was constantly picked on by gang members who believed that he was affiliated with an opposition gang. Turning for him came after having served as a punching bag for members of one gang.

Felix: How did it happen that you joined the Diamonds?

Gustavo: Well, my friends from grammar school were in a gang at my high school, and, since I used to hang out with them, the other gangs began considering me as a member of the gang. The gang itself did not consider me a member, but the other gangs did because they always saw me with these guys. These guys were my friends from grammar school. These were the guys that I grew up with, so I was going to hang out with them.

Felix: Are you saying that at this time you were not an official member of the gang?

Gustavo: No, I wasn't. I became an official member of the gang about three years later, during my junior year in high school.

Felix: What were the reasons for your decision to join the gang then—after all, you were so near graduation?

Gustavo: There were times when I would get into trouble, and the gang would try helping me, but the president of the gang would say that they couldn't do that because I was not an official member. Sometimes I would be chased by another gang because they thought that I was a member of this other gang, and this was happening, and I did not have the protection that other members did. So, finally, I turned. So that, if anything happened to me, I would be protected.

Benjy was having problems at home when he met an older Diamond who inspired him to turn. "Well, I started realizing that me and my parents didn't have this—I can't say we didn't love each other—we didn't have this closeness. I don't know if it was because of my dad's drinking. I can't really put the blame on him or my mom. I can't tell them that it is because of them. But my problems at home confused me a lot. Then, one day I met this guy—I still know him to this day—and he was an older guy. He was maybe twenty-five or twenty-six, and he had been in the gang all his life, since maybe he was eleven years old. He was married with kids; his wife left him; he didn't choose to leave the streets; he chose to stick with it. He recruited me because I was young and the gang needed to expand. So, I joined the gang and started recruiting friends, doing the same thing my friend did to me."

"I met him on a Halloween night, and I was throwing eggs and stuff like that with the guys, doing things that normal teenagers would, but after he came things changed. He started mentioning 'Let's go do this, and let's go shoot up.' He sort of shook [scared] me at first because I never did things that were so criminal. My way of getting back at somebody was like stealing a radio or doing something minor. I was never much of a thief, either. After a while he started teaching me the tricks, how to burn people, how to deal, how to do this, and I made him money. He started turning me on to the gangs, the colors, the hand signals, and everything—how it was done, how you shook someone's hand when you were on the street, and who to eye for. And we became pretty good buddies after about a year and a half."

Once a Diamond, Benjy's affiliation was firmly sealed by rival gang labeling and treatment. "I met my friend during eighth grade. I was still not an official member. Then I started attending high school. Usually, when you're a freshman in high school you feel intimidated by everybody. When you first get to high school you feel like you're taking the first step toward becoming an adult, and I was pretty intimidated by a lot of the students there, and I started fighting back against some of the kids, doing things to people, selling drugs at the school. I remember the first or second day there, a couple of people pointed me out—they knew me from the street—and I remember getting an apple splattered in my face, whipped across from, like, another room. Everyone thought it was funny, so after that I brought golf clubs to school, spray paint, and I started taking charge. I started taking things out physically and violently with other people."

"When you hang around with people and you're seen often by members of another gang, at first they'll say, yeah, maybe he's a friend, but after they see you on the street corner a lot they'll say he is with them. I was just marked, I guess, for the rest of the year, and I guess they were just waiting for me to screw up and do something against one of the enemies of another gang."

═ *Police Treatment*

For other youngsters the way they were handled by the police served as another stimulus for their decision to turn. In the same way that rival gangs take action against neighborhood youngsters they label as belonging to the opposition, the police employ a similar approach. Some members of the Diamonds speak about how the police do not make distinctions when dealing with Latino youngsters from their neighborhood. They are steadily tormented by the police because they appear like gang members or because they are friends with known gang members. In the views of members of the Diamonds all Latino young people, whether they're gang affiliates or not, are targets of a belittling process of police action.

Freddie makes this point very clear as he describes the reasons why he became a member of the Diamonds: "I wasn't a gangbanger. I used to hang out with them; they are my friends. The police started messing with me. They would pull me into their car and harass me. I kept telling them that I was not a banger. But they don't believe anything we tell them. They asked me questions about this and other friends, guys from the hood who are gangbangers, and, since I wouldn't tell them what they wanted to hear, they would say things like, 'Yes, you are one of those hoodlums from this street. We've been watching you for a long time, and now we got you, and you're going to pay.'"

"One day I was with my girlfriend and my friend and his girl—it was the four of us. So we were walking by the neighborhood—this was during Christmas. The police saw us and pulled us over to a corner. They went through their shit—you know, 'Who you be?' 'Where are the other boys?' So, we didn't say nothing. They got really pissed and, in front of our girls, told us to kneel down and sing 'Jingle Bells.' So, there we are singing 'jingle bells, jingle bells, jingle bells' for these pricks. Can you imagine that shit? I wanted to kill them fuckers. How are you supposed to feel when they do that to you for no reason and then in front of your girl? And there's a lot of shit like that that goes on all the time."

"So, one day I told my friends, so we said, 'Well, fuck it. Let's do it.' It seems that we need a fuckin' license to be with our friends. If you're friends with people in a gang, forget it—the law will always be on your case. And to me there is nothing wrong with being friends with these guys; these are the guys I grew up with. We played ball together; we went on picnics together. We did everything together, and now the law comes and says I can't be with them. Well, fuck them. Now that I'm a gangbanger, they have other reasons for messing with me."

Turning for Tony was motivated by several factors; his relations with the police served as a leading one.

Tony: I wouldn't say that I turned because of one thing or the other. I don't believe there is one reason why guys join the gang. We join because of this and that. I joined because I was having problems in school, and then my parents were getting on my case for that, and then the law . . .

Felix: What was happening at home?

Tony: My parents.

Felix: What about them?

Tony: It's a long story. But my parents were getting a divorce. And my mother wanted me with her, and I guess my father didn't like that, so he would come over and put all these ideas in my mind. He be telling things like I was something special and I deserved more than my mother. To tell him what I needed and stuff like that. My mother took me away from the neighborhood because she thought I could do better in some suburb. And I didn't. We moved, and we spent about six months in this suburb, and all that did was to make me more confused. Because I didn't fit in, and I didn't want to fit in. I wanted back to the hood with the guys. We were not bangers. We were just friends. Sometimes you have parents that try to be too protective and that's what happened with mine. They tried to control me all the time. And that doesn't work anymore. Maybe it did for them when they were growing up, but this is different today.

Felix: In terms of the police, what did they do to you?

Tony: There are cops, like Rocky, all right? Rocky is a straight up prick. When my girlfriend was younger Rocky tried to tell her to get in the car. Rocky beat this one homey who had a broken leg right in front of McDonald's one day, with his own crutch. The other day Rocky came up to gangbangers, and he tells them, 'I'm going to bust you,' and then he plants drugs on you. A friend of mine, Tiny, Tiny had a joint on him. One joint. They put it on the record that he had five dimes on him.

Felix: But what did they do to you that has anything to do with you joining the gang?

Tony: They do everything. They take your money when they bust you. They'll go through your wallets saying they're looking for an ID, and the next thing you see is some cops with cash, sticking it in his pocket. Over the years I don't know how much money I've lost to police officers. You know, the people who are supposed to uphold justice—you know, the American way and all this crap—these people rip you off just as much as we do.

Felix: So, they were really messing with you?

Tony: They blame all of this on us, and half the time it's ridiculous. Cops, they lie, and the only difference between them and us is that they have a uniform and a little piece of metal on their chest that says they can get away with this. Some narcs beat the shit out of me and I wasn't a banger. They get away with this. So, I decided if these pricks are going to mishandle me because they think I'm a Diamond I might as well be one. So I did. That's what went down.

Rafael also blames the police for his decision to turn. "The law has always messed with our people. The way they treat us today is not new. This is not something I'm making up. You can ask the older people in the hood. Ask them to tell you about the Puerto Rican riots. I was real little then, but I hear that several cops shot some Puerto Rican kids in the park. Nothing was done to those cops, and they know that they can get away with anything they decide to do to us."

"I was picked up on several occasions by the law because I was Puerto Rican and was walking down the street. I wasn't into gangbanging, but the cops kept asking me about my gang and shit. One time, and this is what really did it for me—after this I decided to turn—I just said fuck it. But, anyway, two white blue boys picked me up and dropped me off in a white neighborhood on the north side. They took my money so I couldn't catch the bus back to the hood. The white dudes from that neighborhood had a field day with me. Well, I tried protecting myself and ran a lot, but I did get the shit smashed out of me. So, what do you do after something like that happens to you? A year ago there were some investigations of blue boys who were picking up black kids and dropping them off in white neighborhoods in the south side or something. Listen, that shit has been happening to us for a long time, and nobody ever gave a shit about it. I didn't want no investigation. Can you imagine the law investigating itself?—in a case involving someone they believe to be a Puerto Rican hoodlum? Well, I resolved it. I turned. I became an official member of the Diamonds, and now they have the right when they stop and ask me questions."

There is also the case of Tomas, who was picked up by two white police officers because he was riding in a car with a couple of his neighborhood friends. "I was in my second year of high school when I got my driver's license. That summer I drove my father's car, and one of my friends, Junior, was also given permission to cruise in his father's ride. One night, about seven or eight, we were cruising through the neighborhood. It was just Junior and me, and we were driving, and these two law dogs pulled us to the side. We were not doing nothing wrong. They told us to get out of the car, and they started searching the car. I asked them what they were doing, and they told us to shut the fuck up. One of them looked at Junior and said, 'Shut up, you little bastard, you spic, we are going to confiscate this car because we know you bought this with dope money.' Junior got charged like hell and told them that the car belonged to my father, that we were not dope dealers. The same cop said to us, 'It doesn't matter. You're gangbangers, we know the gang you belong to, and we plan to destroy it. We are going to harass you until you stop hanging out with your gang friends.' We told them again that we were not bangers, but once again they didn't believe us. This went on for a long time, and finally they took us in. The charge was that we stole the car. After two or three hours at the police station they let us call our parents. Well, by then it was about twelve midnight, and my dad was really pissed. He came to the station to pick us up. The police told him and Junior's dad a bunch of bullshit about us. I didn't drive my father's car again— he didn't let me use it—and, instead, he started accusing me of being a gangbanger. So, I started to identify more and more with the Diamonds. They knew very well about the different ways the law is always trying to set us up—how the police don't care if they break up a family."

"Let me give a better vision of this so you can understand it better. A few days ago on a Saturday, about two in the afternoon, one of my boys, we call him Red because he has red freckles and red hair. . . . Anyway, he was coming from the store with his mother and little brother when the law stopped them. These two big white cops walked over to Red, took a bag he was carrying, and started smacking him. They were hitting him in front of his mother. This cop that nobody likes . . . he kicked Red in the ribs with his flashlight. And, hey, that shit hurts. Anyway, Red's mom became hysterical, and all the law said was that this did not concern her. They also told Red that they had been looking for him for a long time and that he had it coming. After this they got in their mobile and left like if no shit had happened."

"So, you can understand my attitude. This is the way we are treated everyday. Cops don't give a shit who they pick on; after all, we all look the same. We are all bangers to them. There is a war out there; the law has declared war on us. We are targets of abuse for the Chicago police department because they have a license to do what they want. So, if this is how it is going to be, then we have to protect ourselves. I don't have respect for blue boys."

"You know, I didn't have to turn and become a Diamond— these guys knew me for a long time. I grew up together with some of these guys. But I don't regret it now. This is our defense against police brutality."

Clearly, a good part of the lives of members of the Diamonds revolved around the police. Police action made these youngsters feel defenseless and vulnerable in their own neighborhood. They are repeatedly subject to questioning; they are suspected of nearly every crime and made to prove their innocence. Youngsters have come to believe that, as long the police are protected by their status as officials, a system of harassment and dehumanization will persist. And, of course, the deep frustrations youngsters experience in their encounters with the police involve much more than physical fear, time lost, and inconvenience; they are damaging to their human integrity.

These varying accounts point out the very long and complex process youngsters undergo to become official gang members. As Tony indicated, many factors combine to shape the individual's decision to turn. There is no single reason to explain gang participation; however, it is noteworthy that these youngsters' determination to turn was rooted in early childhood experiences.

Flaco, Benjy, Coco, Lobo, and the others were earmarked for failure from day one. They were rejected in "normal" society and labeled as social problems first by the schools and later by the police. This early experience of rejection was devastating; it incapacitated them and broke them, and it denied them their individuality and integrity. To circumvent these consequences these young men sought oppositional forms of resistance. Clearly, for these youngsters the survival behavior that many conventional people consider destructive—participation in a gang—is the one great protection they have against a system in which failure is almost assured.

Intensifying their emerging feelings of antagonism, developed toward their teachers and other school personnel, was the fact that the school was trying to engage them in an almost impossible process of cultural adaptation at the same time they were undergoing the intense identity search of adolescence. During this phase in the socialization process the function of peer culture, shared by those of their kind, superseded all school efforts to mold them according to the latter's predetermined set of standards. The pressure to identify with a culture of resistance, not to reject it, was never greater. In other words, to develop personal identity and maintain integrity these youngsters had to become part of a culture with resistance as its centerpiece. Our mental images and perceptions of gang members do not usually take account of the painful and humiliating road they've traveled to get to where they are.

4

The Diamonds as a Business Enterprise

The day was April 17, 1989. I had just finished having lunch with Rafael in a local restaurant. As we were getting ready to leave, I asked him if I could drive him somewhere, and he said, "I'm going to work. I have to go and make me some bread!" He wanted to be dropped off at the local neighborhood spot where he had been dealing drugs for several years. After being dropped off Rafael and a friend boarded another car, which appeared to have been waiting for him, and drove away, returning nearly thirty minutes later carrying a large amount of merchandise he would try to sell on this day. Once back in the neighborhood he positioned himself alongside other street-level dealers to earn a day's pay. Rafael and his coworkers were employed by one of the Diamonds's distributors, and, like workers in other businesses and professions, they were expected to be at the job for a specified amount of time and to be very productive.

Rafael was the first of the Diamonds I heard refer to his drug-dealing activities in the gang in terms of work. Others tended to describe what they do simply as hanging out or passing the time. Despite the various ways it is referred to, the major activity carried out by members of the Diamonds is street-level dealing, or, as Rafael characterized it, work.

Youngsters' work relations with the gang are a clear illustration of the entrepreneurial nature of the organization—a topic that to date remains unexamined, despite the fairly extensive literature, both scientific and journalistic, available on youth gangs. Most accounts of gangs and drugs tend to associate all teenage drug dealing with the gang; every drug dealer, in this view, is a member of a gang. Of course, this approach overlooks many cases of teenage drug-dealing work which are not affiliated with nor sponsored by the gang. There are some young men, for example, who establish drug-dealing networks, or crews, with several members but, nevertheless, are not a gang; they lack formal organization and a leadership hierarchy and members are not expected to invest time in attending formal meetings nor to pay weekly or monthly monetary contributions or dues. Further, in the eyes of network members the crew does not represent a gang. There are other cases when young people who are not affiliated with the gang manage to develop drug-dealing operations on their own, carrying them out from apartments, known as rock houses, rather than at street level. Others do establish businesses at the street level, though these are independent of gang affiliation and control. There are still other instances of street-level dealing activities conducted by gang members working on their own. (The two latter initiatives are unlikely to materialize where street-level dealing is controlled by the gang, though attempts are made continuously to establish such individual undertakings.)

In any case, in its reporting, the scholarly and journalistic literature does not distinguish between drug dealing that represents a gang activity (or that of its mainheads), wherein a large proportion of the earnings go to the organization, and other kinds of drug dealing which are carried out by those not in a gang, geared to earning money for themselves. The discussion that follows will focus primarily on street-level dealers who work for the gang and who receive a salary for their labor. It will also examine the experiences of several other youngsters who are independent dealers yet still form part of the gang's occupational structure: They purchase their merchandise from the gang's distributors, utilize the gang-controlled turf for retailing, and are required to pay weekly organizational dues.

Several major questions will be considered in the examination. What are the reasons for the gang becoming a business organization? What does the gang look like as an entrepreneurial establishment? That is, what are its defining characteristics as a business enterprise? Which cultural elements are used by youngsters for cementing and reinforcing business relations among themselves? What is the gang's occupational structure? How does the gang generate income for maintaining itself as a business establishment?

═ The Diamonds Become a Business Gang

The history of the Diamonds dates back approximately twenty years, a relatively short period when compared to other Latino youth gangs in Chicago. At first the Diamonds were a musical group, playing their music on street corners in their neighborhood and in local neighborhood nightclubs. Some members believe that in about 1971 a member of the musical group was mistaken for a gang member and was killed by a gunshot fired by a youngster from an opposition gang. This incident sparked the reorganization of the group into a violent criminal youth gang. And for a period of about six years after that the Diamonds were on a course of vengeance and retaliation, provoking intergang fights with other groups.

Spike, a thirty-year member of the Diamonds, who is still very active in the gang, provides a clear description of the early days: "We were a band, and we would play to pass the time, you know, or in some gigs in the neighborhood. This was not one of your well-known professional bands, but we did OK. We were just a bunch of guys who would get together to have fun, to play music in the hood, you know—out on the streets. You know, we were doing the same thing that other people were doing at the park or in basements, except that we were in our hood. Then the band started to attract followers, people from the neighborhood that liked the music, and they would be there all the time. These people were like bodyguards, you know, to make sure that the band was safe. So the group started growing, and then, all of the sudden, there was talk about forming the group into a gang, so some of them decided to do it. These were the followers and not the band. I don't know what was the problem with some of these guys; maybe one of them had a run-in with the opposition. We never knew the whole story. But, anyway, it was about this time when one of the band players got shot. So, from here on they decided to become a gang and keep the name of the Diamonds, you know, the name of the band. And for a long time they were hard-core, you know—these guys were mean motherfuckers.

You couldn't go by the neighborhood because they were shooting at everybody. It was really bad. It was worse than what these guys are doing today. There were times we would have these wars with the opposition, and we go out to the park, the two gangs, with bats, clubs, guns, and shit, and just have it out right there. It was crazy. I can tell you of about ten guys from our side who died from gang fights. Some of the fights were right here because the opposition would drive by shooting at us. Some of our guys got killed right here."

During most of this early period the membership of the Diamonds was quite small; the organization had not expanded and divided itself into sections. Gang members' involvement with drugs—in particular, marijuana—was essentially for their own recreational use. The Diamonds had yet to become a profit-making business enterprise. In some instances, a member would purchase a relatively sizable amount of marijuana and sell to others in the gang. Sometimes money was collected to purchase a quantity of marijuana, which would be equally distributed among contributing members, again, most of the drug was for personal and, at times, social use. As indicated by Spike, while describing the early days of the gang, "We would just get high a lot. It seemed that everybody was doing drugs at that time. It's not like today where people are trying to prevent drug use. No, before there used to be stories about movie stars smoking reefer and doing coke, and they were cool and bad. Doctors were doing drugs; attorneys were doing drugs. I tell you, everybody was doing it. So, we started doing it, too. There were the fights between us and some other gangs—that's another thing we used to do. But, besides that, we would be drinking beer and doing drugs. We were not selling drugs at this time. What we did was to buy the drugs and use them ourselves. We still did not know enough to go into business. We didn't know where to sell them, except for to our friends, who were already one of us."

Then, in the late 1970s, a major change occurred in the operational structure of the Diamonds. It began to take on a businesslike character. No longer were retaliative, violent behavior against opposition gangs and reefer smoking the mainstays of the organization. Money-making through drug dealing came to represent the gang's emerging chief function. Although a great deal of gangbanging persisted as the Diamonds and enemy gangs maintained ongoing feuds, overall the gang embraced and carried out a program that was built around money-making activities.

Why did the Diamonds undergo this change during this particular period? Which factors and conditions were responsible for the transformation?

Controlled Substance Act

"I remember this older guy from the neighborhood who wanted me to sell for him. He asked several of us to be his dealers. He was offering good money, but I was afraid. I didn't know what he was about. We knew that he was doing something because all these people used to come to his house all the time. Hey, like some of us guys sometimes went to him to cop some smokes for us. He was offering us some good money. He said that we could work for him and that he was going to take care of us. He was even talking about cars; you know, if you do real good and if you're reliable, you know, all of that shit, that he would buy us a beamer [BMW]. And that we would not have to worry again about buying smokes because we would have it all the time. But since he had never dealt with us before and then all of sudden he wanted us to work for him, I was scared. I said not to the buy, I couldn't trust the cat."

What Carmelo is describing is in larger terms an event that had a major influence on the business development of the gang—namely, a piece of legislation; the Illinois Controlled Substance Act, which was passed in 1971 and carried heavy criminal penalties for adult heroin and cocaine dealers. The bill called for mandatory twenty-year prison sentences for drug peddling offenders eighteen years and older.

Well aware that juveniles could always beat the penalties of the newly instituted law, those adults who for the most part had controlled drug distribution and dealing up to this point began enlisting some of the youngsters from the Diamonds as well as from other gangs to work the street blocks and corners of particular neighborhoods. Some youngsters, like Carmelo, refused the job offers, while others agreed to them. It did not take some of these youngsters or leaders of the gang very long to realize, however, that they could profit substantially by controlling neighborhood drug dealing. In other words, these young people began to ask the question "If this is our neighborhood and people are using it to make money, why can't we develop our own business?"

And, indeed, they did. Gang leaders began reorganizing the structure of the Diamonds into a wholesale enterprise or investment; the organization became a business establishment. It now purchased wholesale merchandise itself and hired its own members, especially the younger ones, to retail at the street level. Since the Diamonds viewed themselves as landlords of several *puntos* in the neighborhood (literally translated, the word *punto* stands for "points," but here it refers to street corners), the only missing ingredient for developing a business operation was the necessary capital with which to purchase large amounts of drugs for extracting a profit.

Felix: You said that, when the gang got involved in the drug business, you started from scratch. What did you mean by that?

Spike: Well, we did not know anything about the business. We didn't have any money.

Felix: Why didn't you work with some of the people who were already established dealers?

Spike: You mean the dealers, the older guys?

Felix: Yes, those guys.

Spike: Well, like, they were not with us. They were not part of the organization. We saw them like the competition.

Felix: So, what did you do with these guys?

Spike: Don't get me wrong—these guys were powerful. They had all the money. What we did was to take control of the neighborhood, you know, to make it ours.

Felix: How did you do that?

Spike: Well, we were not allowed to work for them. And we started to control dealing from the streets. If you want to deal from the street, you got to be part of us or you can't do it. If you try, we take the shit from you or simply beat the shit out of the guy. That was our neighborhood, so we decided to run our business from there. We wanted to control what was ours.

Felix: What happened to the older guys?

Spike: I don't know, maybe they sold from their house or in their business. For some of these guys there's a lot of money in selling drugs to big-time people—you know, like doctors, lawyers, you know, people in big business.

Not one individual within the Diamonds organization possessed the necessary capital for purchasing large enough quantities of drugs for turning a profit. No single member had the money necessary for establishing himself as the sole owner or shareholder of the corporation. Therefore, some members began pooling their money: Sometimes two or three of the older members (usually the leaders, or chiefs) would "go into business"; at other times the group of investors was larger. On other occasions leaders would command all members to make an investment of a certain minimum amount (along with the lines of passing the hat) and would use this sum for purchasing the necessary amount of drugs with which to start the business. And in still other situations leaders of the gang would simply take and use the dues money for the purchase of large amounts of drugs.

Spike recounts this initial stage in the business development of the Diamonds: "At first it was real tough because we didn't have any cash. So, we would try different ways to raise enough to make a profit. You know, we would all chip in; you know there was no hassle about the money or stuff like that. We wanted the business to get off the ground, you know, make it work because we didn't have nothing for us. This was going to be something that was going to be ours, you know, for us. And once we got going we took control. But at first it was real difficult. And then we had to make sure that people did not spend gang money on themselves. So, it took a little while to get going. But we knew that there was a lot of money to be made in this business. This was a business made for us; it was something like it was sent by God. It was a business that we could do straight from the neighborhood that we controlled and knew real well. How could you go wrong?"

To the question "Who controlled the money made from dealing?" Spike answered, "It always was the chief or mainheads. They were the leaders. They had earned their position, and we respected them, and we had a lot of trust in them. So when we paid dues we knew that it was our money, but, in fact, it was the gang's money. And, since the chiefs and mainheads were the leaders, it was the same as the gang. That's how we used to see it then."

High Demand for Drugs

The rise of the economic side of the gang was also aided by the increasing demand for drugs—in particular, cocaine—caused by the spiraling popularity of drug use in the United States during the 1970s and the blossoming international cocaine trade. The streets of the city became flooded with huge amounts of drugs as Chicago came to represent a central distribution point for the international drug trade. One distributor reflects on earlier times when he was a street-level dealer, when he would sell his merchandise so quickly that at times some customers were left without goods—that is, the demand was greater than the supply.

Felix: How would you compare selling now to years ago?

Carmelo: I was dealing in the streets back in 1974 or so. We did not have the organization that we have now. Now we deal through the gang. So, that was one difference.

Felix: What was another difference?

Carmelo: I think it was the amount of bo [marijuana] and powder [cocaine], but mainly bo, that were out in the streets. Cocaine was expensive, but bo . . . everybody wanted it, and we were making bo-gu [beaucoups: French term used as slang, meaning "a lot of"] cash.

Felix: How was that possible?

Carmelo: Like I told you, there was a lot of stuff out there. There were times when I would get my supply in the morning and then go back in the afternoon and get some more. My supplier wanted me out there all the time because the stuff was selling real fast. There were times when I had to turn some of my customers on to somebody else—something I never wanted to do—but if I didn't have the stuff it was better that they cop from other guys. That way they would not want to stop using it. That's what kept us going. Yeah, but, man, that was good. . . . Today, well, you seen how that is.

Felix: And how is it today?

Carmelo: Well, sometimes we got to chill out because of the law. I don't think that people are using as much. And then things get dried up. You know, because of all the busting, you know, the law is out there to bust people and take their shit. So, when that happens things are really slow.

Felix: Where did your supplier get the stuff from?

Carmelo: Different places. I know that there was a runner who used to pick up reefer and even cocaine from this one man. I think that he was the main supplier. And that was here in the neighborhood. Then there were these other dudes I remember seeing a couple one time. I don't know where they were from. But I know that they had money; they had all kinds of jewelry on them, bad cars—you know, the works. The stuff was everywhere.

Felix: Were these people Puerto Ricans?

Carmelo: I don't know. For sure they were Latinos. The ones that were from the neighborhood—I went to their crib one time. One time I went to one of their parties that my chief invited me to. It was me, my chief, and several other people. These guys lived in luxury. This was at an apartment, not their house. And they had all these women and furniture and waterbeds and a bar; it was something else, like one of these things you see on TV. These guys had it all. They were the rich and famous.

For Angel, who has been a street-level dealer since becoming a Diamond in 1977, the experience was very similar. "Actually, those were the good old days," he recalls. "People would come to your corner looking for you. You didn't have to be waving hand signals at nobody. They would pull over at any time of the day. And I didn't have to force anybody to buy my stuff. We only did that later when there was a lot of competition. But, before, there wasn't so many of these sections that you have today. Today a gang could have ten sections, and they all be selling. But, before, the customers were there all the time. It was like . . . there was this hunger for drugs. I don't know who controlled the supply, but, then, when our boys started buying the stuff themselves and bringing it we all started doing real good, ten times better than what I'm doing today."

"I think one thing that had us really scared was that there was so much stuff out there we were afraid our boys would start using a lot and getting hooked. That would had been real bad for the business. And we all know that a couple of guys flipped. They got involved. They started using, and when we found out what they were doing we tried to make them stop, but they could always go to another section to get stuff. And sometimes, because they were one of us, they got stuff on credit. And, because there were was so much of the shit out there, the dealers started trusting people and giving them the shit so they could pay later. To me that was bad business. But you got to remember that I'm talking about the time when there was a lot of stuff—everybody had some. So, to get rid of it they would do all kinds of things."

"For our boys, those fellas that started using, they knew that if we threw them out of the business they could go some other places to cop. And they did. And then they did this until they got into trouble with the law."

The Nation Coalition

In early spring 1990 a Puerto Rican youth from Division Street was shot by another who was a riding a Chicago Transit Authority bus. The young man died almost instantaneously. Every major television station and city newspaper reported the shooting, defining it as a gang-related murder. It was another in a series of bloody incidents that had wounded the hearts of residents of the northwest side.

A day later I informed a couple of the Diamonds of the shooting. I was interested in learning their views about it. They were already aware of what had happened. Rafael said, "Oh, that was a guy from another nation. Those boys are at war with one another. I think that they are breaking their nation." I asked him what was the meaning of this concept of nation, and he said, "My understanding of what the nation means is that we are supposed to respect other groups from the same nation." I asked him to elaborate further, to which he agreed, and said, "Gangbanging is nothing really hard to do. In my neighborhood you have to hang out a lot. Our chief wants us out there a lot so nobody else would try to take our neighborhood from us. And we have boundaries, and a little bit of the neighborhood we have to share with others from the same nation but of a different affiliation. And we have our territory, and, if they were to come into our territory, we wouldn't start trouble by getting loud and stuff like that. We all respect each other pretty much, and it's alright."

At a more general level Rafael's remarks serve to characterize the relatively cooperative and congenial relations established by rival gangs in Chicago in the early 1980s—a multigang peaceful settlement helped into place by the division of city areas into two gang nations, or alliances; People and Folks. (Suburbia's various gangs came under the sponsorship of the Folks.) Gangs belonging to the same nation were expected not to engage in fights and squabbles. It was expected that relations between nation-member gangs were to be nonviolent. If fights were to erupt, they were to be directed at opposition gangs—that is, against gangs from the other nation. No one is really certain of the lineage of the national alliance, but it is rumored that this alignment was formed by incarcerated members of rival gangs in 1981. It is also believed that jailed, former leaders of these two parent groups continue to play a significant role in dictating the policies and actions of street gangs in Chicago.

Theoretically, the nation approach was directed at significantly reducing the degree of intergang violence which had been so prevalent during the 1970s in the city and had led not only to numerous killings but also to the development of several anti-gang initiatives by local neighborhood residents, parents, and police. Several major structures and organizations were created to combat and exterminate gang activities. As a measure aimed at derailing these efforts, the nation arrangement was reached. As Rafael indicated, under the nation agreement gangs belonging to the same coalition were discouraged from invading each other's territories, while at the same time agitation and harassment were to be avoided by coalition members.

And, indeed, organizing various gangs into a nation was good for business: It contributed immensely to solidifying the business operation of the gang. "Respect for each other's territories" also came to mean the sharing of the larger drug consumer market. There was a clear understanding that the consumer drug market was immeasurably wide, enabling the various gangs to have their own shares without having to fight and compete with the others. Each gang could now run its business operations within a relatively safe turf, or marketplace, selling only to those customers who voluntarily frequented it. No longer was the gang involved in efforts to take over other hoods, hoping to expand its business boundaries beyond its immediate neighborhood setting. In addition, the reduction in gangbanging activity, ordained by the nation agreement, helped immensely to improve the image and reputation of the business turf, furnishing consumers with a safe and protective "shopping environment." The chances of being caught in the middle of intergang controversies were reduced, the neighborhood was made to be more safe for consumer spending.

To suggest that members of the Diamonds are committed to relations of mutual understanding and harmony with other gangs is not to claim a total absence of intergang conflict. In fact, members of the Diamonds believe that the nation alliance has broken down in recent times as gangbanging among nation gangs becomes routine. But the significant point is that, at first, the nation alliance reduced intergang violence substantially, apparently enough to enable some gangs to establish their organizations on sound business terms.

Perceptions of Conventional Work

Youngsters' images of "traditional" jobs were perhaps the leading force that helped to transform the gang into a business venture. These young men began turning to the gang in search of employment opportunities, believing that available conventional work would not sufficiently provide the kinds of material goods they wished to secure. Some of the more common assessments I heard about conventional work available for Latino youth are captured in the following two expressions:

There are some jobs that people can still find, but who wants them? They don't pay. I want a job that can support me. I want a job that I could use my talents—speaking, communicating, selling, and a definite goal that I'd be working toward as far as money is concerned.

We were just tired of factory jobs. We were supposed to go to school and receive an education. For what? To be employed in factory jobs? We were tired of that. At the same time we were watching these other guys making a lot of money, so we said, 'Hey, let's follow these guys. Let's do what they were doing."

These remarks also allow us to gain insight into the pessimistic outlook these young people have developed toward job prospects in the regular economy. Members of the Diamonds have become increasingly convinced that the jobs available to them are essentially meaningless, far from representing the vehicles necessary for overcoming societal barriers to upward mobility. Although these youngsters have been socialized with a view to the conventional cultural course to achieving material success, they refuse to buy into its official means. That is, they do not agree to accept the "American achievement ideology," representative of middle-class norms and shown by Horowitz (1983), Kornblum (1985), and others to be widely supported by ethnic and racial minority parents and teenagers. The ideology stresses that success in school leads to the attainment of managerial and professional jobs, which, in turn, pave the way for social and economic advancement. The youngsters' own school experiences and occasional contacts with the job market—as well as their observations of the frustrating and often futile efforts by some adults around them to achieve social advancement through menial, dead-end jobs—combine to serve as overwhelming evidence that the American achievement ideology does not necessarily apply to them. In brief, these young men do not believe in the power of education to be the "great equalizer" nor do they see existing "legitimate work" as capable of leading them to a successful, meaningful life.

The views of these young people point out the poignant paradox between having culturally defined goals and ineffective but socially legitimate means for achieving them, indicated by sociologist Robert Merton several decades ago and since confirmed by researchers and scholars writing on gangs, youth, and employment (Vigil 1988; Kornblum 1987; Horowitz 1983; Moore 1978; Cloward and Ohlin 1960). The contradiction lies in the absence of avenues and resources necessary for securing the rewards that society most values and which it purports to offer its members.

The decision by members of the Diamonds to accept participation in the gang is informed by their assessments of the lack of available opportunities in the regular economy but also by their high level of aspirations. Rather than arising as a deliberate violation of middle-class aspirations, the gang represents a "counter-organization," a response geared to fulfilling the standards of the larger society. The transformation of the gang into a business enterprise was sparked by the will to change, to alter those forces of domination weighing heavily upon its members' lives. In effect, what these youngsters did was reconstruct the "criminal" gang into an income-generating business operation—an alternate form of employment with which they could hope to "make it" in U.S. society. In the words of Spike, "We grew up at a time when people were making money and making it quick. You know, we saw on television people getting rich overnight. You had the professional athletes—these are the guys who are supposed to have natural talents, you know. That's a lot of bullshit. It's true these guys were taking steroids. You had all these reports about how these athletes were pumping iron and taking steroids so they could sell their bodies and so people could pay to watch them. That's one thing we saw. Then we saw, you know, you had the white-collar criminals—you know, those guys who are just like us but never get caught, except that everybody knows that they are crooks. You had all these guys becoming filthy rich. And what do you think that's going to tell us? Shit, it didn't tell me to go and get a job at McDonalds and save my nickels and dimes. Who the fuck was doing it that way? Who the fuck is saving nickels and dimes today? You have kids coming up to you today and asking you for a buck, not for a nickel or a dime or a quarter. Where do they see this shit? You tell me. I wasn't going to save my nickels and dimes. That certainly wasn't going to be me because I would still be waiting, and I would be the only one waiting. Things are not done like that anymore. So, we decided to turn to what we have, and that was us."

"Some of us fucked up. We didn't make it. I'm thirty years old, and I'm still out here hustling everyday. But that's because certain things didn't work out the way I wanted. I'm not going to make excuses for my mistakes. But you know what? I'm going to continue because there are many people like me, people who have jobs, people who are making only enough to pay the rent, and then they come out here or go into other kinds of illegal business because they know that what society says and gives them are two different things."

— Social and Cultural Components of the Ethnic Enterprise

What are the distinguishing characteristics of the gang which enable it to function as a business organization—a type of establishment necessarily built around a great deal of trust and commitment, which allow it to generate and sustain consistent and dependable social relations and monetary gains? That is, which social and cultural elements did the youngsters use for organizing the gang into a reliable money-making enterprise?

In the same way that the family unit teaches its young the norms, skills, values, beliefs, and traditions of the larger society, the gang has developed its own culture, including its own myths, norms, values, and ways of communicating and reinforcing them. At the heart of the gang culture is a collective ideology that serves as the basis for realizing the overall welfare of all the members. For the gang collectivism is the major determinant of its efficient development as a business operation. The members' responses to their shared conditions and circumstances are collective in the sense that they lead to partnership, therefore uniting many individuals.

For the members of the Diamonds collectivism translates into an ideology of strength. These young men share the belief that their capacity to make a living or improve their life chances can only be realized through a "collective front." In Coco's view, "We are a group, a community, a family—we have to learn to live together. If we separate, we will never have a chance. We need each other even to make sure that we have a spot for selling our supply. You know, there is people around here, like some opposition, that want to take over your *negocio* [business]. And they think that they can do this very easy. So we stick together, and that makes other people think twice about trying to take over what is yours. In our case, the opposition has never tried messing with our hood, and that's because they know it's protected real good by us fellas."

Rafael echoes Coco's interpretation of collectivism: "Together we have the numbers. We have protection. My business is his business because we protect our interests together. So we talk about our thing—it's nobody's thing; rather, it's our thing. I think that one of the first things we learn when we start off is to feel like a group or a family. That means that we have to share and we have to protect each other and whatever belongs to us." In effect, though gang members can (and in some cases do) pursue individual financial gains, their business ventures are made possible because of the gang, and their individual work is geared to enhancing the common good and to pursuing collective ends.

The collectivist nature of the gang can be said to be an extension of the traditional Puerto Rican family. In Puerto Rican immigrant society, as well as in other societies from which ethnic and racial groups in the United States originated, the family served as the cornerstone of the culture, defining and determining individual and social behavior. Ties between families were cemented by the establishment of *compadrazco* (godparent-godchild) relationships. Relatives by blood and ceremonial ties as well as friends of the family were linked together in an intricate network of reciprocal obligations. Individuals who suffered misfortunes were aided by relatives and friends, and when these individuals had reestablished themselves they shared their good fortunes with those who had helped them.

That the gang is rooted in the norms of conventional family life and tradition can be observed from the various descriptions of the gang offered by some of the Diamonds's members.

Tony: My grandmother took care of me for a long time. I guess this was part of the Puerto Rican tradition at one time. Your grandmother took care of you while your mother and father were away working. Sometimes grandmothers did not believe that their son or daughter were fit to be parents so they took the responsibility of raising their grandchildren. My grandmother lived with us, and to me she is my life. Anybody who messes with my grandmother has to mess with me. The same thing with my aunt.

Felix: Which aunt are you referring to?

Tony: This is my mother's sister, which is really weird because they are the same blood but treat me so differently. My aunt is the mother I never had. My mother tried raising me to be a real good boy—you know, one of those kids who don't go out into the streets and who is always studying. That's difficult to do

when you are raised in Chicago. So, she wasn't understanding. But my aunt was. We are really close. She is the person
that I go to when I need someone to tell something to. She
always listens to me.

Felix: And why does she always listen to you?

Tony: My aunt is this wonderful woman—she's about thirty-
five years old—who is really together. When I'm with her I
feel like I can tell her anything that is on my mind. That's
what family is all about. This is all in the blood. She cares
because she is family. When you have a family, even if it's
your aunt or uncle, you know you belong. You will always
have someone looking out for you.

Felix: In the last interview you talked a little about the family as
it related to the gang. How similar is the gang family to what
you're describing now?

Tony: They are very similar. You see a family is like a fist [he
points to his fist, clenching it and opening it to show that
when it's opened it represents five fingers separated from
one another]. I know that the five fingers of your hand are
supposed to be related; however, what would you prefer
having, a hand with five fingers or a closed fist? When the fist
is closed the fingers are inseparable; when the fist is opened
they stand at a distance from one another. I prefer the closed
fist. That's exactly how our gang is; we are very closed. To be in
our gang you need to have heart. To have heart means that you
are truly committed to each other; that you'll do anything for
another member because he is part of your family.

Lobo's reply when queried about his relationship with other
gang members is illustrative and provides another good sum-
mary of the gang as a family unit: "I would say belonging with
them for so many years, all day and every day—that's what
makes a family. When you get ready to leave a gang you must go
through this stage where you get beat up. I didn't. My friends,
those that were there by my side and I was by theirs for a long
time, they couldn't do it. They couldn't beat on me. They were
the ones who stood back and said, 'I'm not gonna to do it. Get
someone else.' So the ones they got to jump on me were from a
different section of the gang. . . . I remember one guy said, 'He's
like a brother to me. I'm not going to hit him. And, if this means
that I have to stand by him so you guys could hit him, well, go
ahead and hit me, too.' For him to say that—that had to be from
love, from being brothers for so long in the gang."

In addition to its stemming directly from a Puerto Rican family tradition, ethnic solidarity served as another fundamental cultural element, used by the youngsters for cementing their business relations. As Puerto Ricans, they expressed feelings of a fundamental tie (blood, or kinship, solidarity), believed to represent a major unifying force. Of course, this organic bond, in turn, provided the basis for trust. One explanation about the correlation between ethnicity and group solidarity was offered by Rafael: "The fact that I knew that what I liked was at another person's house—they would talk to me about things like, 'We're going to listen to Salsa music, we're going to have *arroz con candules* [rice and potpies]' and some other stuff—I would get more attracted to that than to other things. That brought us more together. And that's how things are with other people from other nationalities. Polish people—have you been over where they have all the stores not far from here? Well, they have their own neighborhood and groups, you know, like they do their own thing together. So, we do our thing together, too, as one people. We have our hood, our own Latino stores and the business we do in our gang works because we are the same people. We trust each other because we understand what we are all about."

In Flaco's view, "It was easy for us to get tight because, as Puerto Ricans, we have an understanding about different things that is the same. You know, as Puerto Ricans growing up together we go through the same things. We notice that we all are treated the same way by everybody. You know, our people have more problems in school, with the police, than any other group. So, we ask ourselves, What's going on? So, now we are using ourselves—you know, the things we like doing and believe in—to keep us really together. There were times when our families would get together, not as gangs but as families, and would have picnics. For us this was almost natural because, as Puerto Ricans, we knew what we were all about. It's different when you are with your own."

It is clear that the collectivist, communitarian underpinning of the gang was also buttressed by a base of local consumers. Their willingness to become faithful customers, to continuously purchase available goods—drugs and stolen merchandise—is viewed by those in the gang as an indication of a sort of surrogate membership in the gang. Additionally, customers protect gang members working as street-level dealers by agreeing to withhold information when interrogated by police officers and other law enforcement agents. These customers become, in the opinion of one youngsters, "one of us." Flaco elaborated on this point: "People from the neighborhood know that they can get smoke, caine, and other things from us. It's risky going to other places. They don't know what those other people be about. So they protect us because they feel secure with us. And we are safe with them. So, we think of them as part of the business."

These various sources of collective behavior are thought to have played a leading role in cementing the Diamonds's business structure. The significance of collectivism for gang members can also be gleaned from their views about the idea of individualism. These youngsters do not agree with the view that the exercise of individual effort in pursuit of economic and social mobility applies to them. To them individualism means placing oneself in a precarious position: How can they survive without one another? They are fully aware that they do not possess the traditional resources, such as money and high levels of formal education, used by members of the middle class to negotiate and advance their individual life chances.

To them individual behavior leads to obliteration. Tony makes the claim that "by ourselves we are nobody." He says, "We can be had without no problem. I'm always with my partners because when you're by yourself you are easy prey. You are going to fall to the bottom of the barrel because, well, who's going to be there for you? So, if people come at you as a bunch, then we need to create our bunch." Other of Tony's remarks are just as straightforward: "This is not a game that you can win by yourself. If you want to win, you do it as a team. We call ourselves a family, but, you know, when you really think about it we're also a team. And, if you want to lose, play alone. Most of our guys who fall, they fall because they sometimes do things without thinking. Sometimes just do stupid things. You know, sometimes they go on their own and end up losing. Myself, I have gotten busted by the police several times because I was alone. I couldn't see them coming. When you're with your boys you have more eyes to check out what's going on—you can see the cops; you can see the opposition. But when you are by yourself sometimes you feel scared, and you know that there is so much you see and so much you can do. In the Diamonds we teach the young guys; we practice how to be together all the time. We think that that's our strength. Other people have money. We have each other."

One other major reason for rejecting the individualist stance is that these young people recognize that success in U.S. society, which is structured around the concept of individualism, has one major interpretive implication: As success honors those who have achieved it, failure (and economic failure in particular) stigmatizes those who suffer it. The system, thus, makes those who have "failed" the objects of criticism and scorn. It can also imply that one's inadequacies in the social system are based upon some innate deficiency; failure thus evokes pity and concern. The emphasis on the individual in gauging success and failure in U.S. society is unacceptable as far as these young men are concerned. For this reason they see collectivism as a way of giving gang members a special sense of purpose—the driving force with which to pursue economic and social success.

= Rules of Collectivism

It is well understood that the business success of the Diamonds is heavily dependent upon its capacity to engender a feeling of collectivism among members. A major responsibility of the gang is to encourage this behavior, and it has employed several methods to guarantee that its members' thinking and work practices proceed within a collectivist context.

Individual members of the gang who decide to work on their own are fully aware of the severe penalties associated with such behavior if it leads to problems with the law. Members who are apprehended by the police, for example, for selling drugs or stealing on their own may not be entitled to receiving the amenities accorded to those who engage in collective action. Elf, who spent several months in jail, describes the consequences of working alone: "I was left to rot. My people didn't come for me. We were all warned about doing shit by ourselves. I was one who paid for not listening. Sometimes you do things without thinking—everybody does, right?—but, then, when you get caught doing some stupid shit that's when you start thinking and paying attention to what you're doing. I was away for a long time—hey, six months is a long time—when I could have come out in a few days."

Additionally, individual action can lead to severe physical harm—in particular, the brutal punishment embellished in the violation ritual—as happened to Carmelo on more than one occasion. "At one time, well, sometimes we get greedy and do things by ourselves so we won't have to share with others. And we need to do it this way because sometimes we need things real bad, like, you know, you might need money for your rent or to buy food, and then you get dumb. That's what happened to me. I needed to pay some bills, so I came out here one day and did my thang. But the law grabbed me real quick. They took all the shit I had, so the mainhead lost a lot of money. So, you know what happened. They got me out and used me as an example. So, they called a meeting and told everybody to be there. They wanted to set an example. I got a violation, and they did me real good."

"Then another time I got another violation for spray-painting the opposition wall because they saw me doing it, and then we got into a war with those guys. The war lasted for several months, and that wasn't cool because we were not making no cash since we were fighting and we were supposed to be ready for the opposition. And because I did this without an order from the chief, I was given another V. We just don't go and spray peoples' walls by ourselves or without permission. Some people do it, but if they get caught, like what happened to me, then they got to pay."

Conversely, members of the Diamonds have been taught to recognize the advantage of functioning as a collectivity rather than as individuals. As gang members, street-level dealers, for example, are offered a fairly safe marketplace in which to sell their products. The Diamonds's hood, the location in the neighborhood where drug transactions tend to occur, is reserved for use by members only. In cases when a particular turf has developed a reputation for carrying stocks of reliable and good merchandise, as is true for the turf of the section of the Diamonds I studied, youngsters can be almost guaranteed of having an ongoing clientele—that is, a profitable business.

Another advantage of a collectivist approach to doing business is found in the symbolic messages this action tends to communicate, to "outsiders" in particular. The presence of a group of dealers on a street block, for example, usually taking turns to ensure that everyone has an opportunity to make a sale, serves to discourage possible robbery attempts. Customers, users and others not associated with the gang, recognize the inherent risk in trying to burglarize a group of dealers who are working together and known to be members of a particular gang. In addition, the gang provides individuals with a reputation, serving as a safeguard against possible customer snitching; that is, customers and other individuals would be hesitant and fearful to reveal information about a particular dealer who is known to belong to a particular gang. There is widespread understanding that to snitch against one dealer is commensurate with revealing information about the entire gang, an act youngsters in the streets know will engender retribution and a great deal of physical violence.

The gang, as representative of a collective unit, carries another advantage. It provides customers with a reputable source from which to purchase drugs and other items, and, in doing so, it contributes significantly to cementing seller-customer relations. Knowledge about the gang, its territory, its affiliated dealers, and its overall reputation gives customers the background information necessary to trust that the merchandise they buy is authentic and first-rate. Customers feel confident about not being sold a fraudulent product, or what street-level dealers call "junk." After all, customers know where to locate sellers. In the words of Red, "The Diamonds have a good reputation. We get people buying our stuff from everywhere. There are people from the suburbs that know who we are. They know that our stuff is the best. Hey, I bet that some of these cats have bought some junk from other turfs. Our reputation tells them that this is where it's at."

Finally, the collective approach to selling drugs provides youngsters with defense against police invasion and apprehension. The different members of the Diamonds, employed as street-level dealers, carry out their job responsibilities in groups, or crews, of at least three members—a work arrangement aimed at offering reliable protection. Organization of street-level dealers into work crews is helpful for keeping each worker alert and informed about the different threats surrounding him—in particular, the police. Having to conduct an "illegitimate" business from an open and highly visible location, such as a street corner, makes for easy seizure by the police. (This issue is discussed further in the following chapter.)

Occupational Character

The Diamonds's money-making operation is built around a fairly elementary, hierarchical occupational structure. Several leading jobs exist within this occupational pyramid: drug suppliers/distributors, cocaine and marijuana dealers, and jobs involving several forms of stealing. Like other business establishments, the gang's hierarchical structure represents an ordered arrangement of power, prestige, authority, and information. One's position on the pyramid is related to one's access to and possession of these attributes.

At the top level of the gang's occupational hierarchy stand

the cocaine and marijuana suppliers, or distributors. The number of suppliers/distributors is limited to a handful, for the smaller the total number, the larger the potential profit. Members of the Diamonds refer to their distributors/suppliers as "leaders," "older guys," "chiefs," or simply "mainheads."

The distributor epitomizes success within the gang; by his lofty status he seduces newer members. He is not an illusion but a flesh and blood man, and he represents the dream that many gang members believe the larger society has denied most Puerto Rican youngsters like themselves. In the minds of these members the distributor represents the position within the business infrastructure of the gang they hope to achieve. Red views his distributor in a positive light, yet he remains convinced that he will not be able to reach this level in the gang occupational hierarchy, at least not soon enough. He says, "I would see my prez [chief] and other mainheads, you know, with two or three cars, and this and that, and they still got jobs, money. You see a bankroll in their pocket, and they be asking you what you want to eat. They be asking you this and that, and you be like, 'I want to make this money and that money. I want to be like you.' And he'll be like, 'OK, well, I'll go and buy an ounce of bo for you, right, 'cause you ain't got the money to do it.' And you know you can't do it. I mean, how many of the guys make it to the top? The number is really small because they tell you or give you all these things to do and sell because they know how far you can get. These guys are not stupid."

For sure, the distributor position is not open to most members of the gang; it is a fairly closed, or exclusive, club. The few individuals who remain with the gang long enough to achieve this level are usually mandated to create a new section of the gang (a new business turf) in a different area of the neighborhood. In other cases they are simply appointed to an existing section viewed by the leadership as impotent, or nonproductive, for failing to have generated a sound financial base. Lobo provides a precise account of the nature of the job of the distributor: "In my section the big guys would never change. They were the distributors—the people everybody wanted to be like—but it was very hard to get their positions. They had the control and were not going to give it to anyone. If you got big like them, you had to work with another section. They didn't let you compete with them. Why should they? They were going to lose money. But I guess it's not a bad idea to create your section—it's only yours."

Most workers within the job hierarchy of the Diamonds occupy the position of street-level cocaine and marijuana dealers— the job directly beneath that of distributor/supplier. In most cases dealers sell both drugs, though the preference is for the cocaine business for its larger potential profits. Dealing cocaine and marijuana requires available cash in order to purchase the drug from the supplier; otherwise, youngsters work as sellers for the supplier, who "fronts" them a certain amount of drugs. Dealers receive a small percentage of the profits. There are other times when the supplier uses gang members to sell cocaine and marijuana by hiring them to make "drops," or deposits, of specific amounts to individuals outside of the neighborhood; the profits from this job are also usually small.

Finally, at the bottom of the gang's occupational hierarchy are those youngsters who make money through stealing. The large number of youngsters involved in acts of stealing are the newer members, called the "Pee Wees" or "Littles." In many cases, stealing represents a "special mission" Pee Wees are instructed to carry out to demonstrate their loyalty and commitment to the gang. Although these efforts are intended to let new members "prove themselves," they manage to generate a profit. For some youngsters, however, stealing becomes a way of life. They work in crews of three or four, and the major item they target is cars. These youngsters become extremely competent in stealing cars and can make a substantial amount of money from it, though not near as much as that generated from street-level drug dealing.

Money-raising Capacity

Similar to other business organizations, the gang's survival is heavily dependent on its capacity to develop and maintain a sound financial base. Funds are needed for meeting a wide range of organizational needs, such as the purchase of weapons, making rent payments, bailing members out of jail, and paying for attorney's fees. The gang's finances are secured primarily through two major sources: one is the organization's own centralized fund, referred to by youngsters as the "box," and, the other, the private funds of drug suppliers within the gang.

The centralized fund, or box, is established mainly through membership contributions, paid regularly to the gang's treasurer. As Eddie explained, "Without the kiddy [box] we would have disappeared a long time ago. We needed all kinds of money to bail heads out of the joint because for a while we were doing some heavy gangbanging. We were paying about ten to fifteen dollars a week."

The significance of membership dues in maintaining the gang on a sound financial basis is described in detail by another young man:

Felix: How often did you pay dues in your gang?

Hector: We pretty much paid twice a month. We were paying ten to twenty dollars per crack. To me that was a lot of cash. When you add that together that's a lot of cash. We had about forty guys, so add it up.

Felix: What would have happened if you didn't pay?

Hector: But we had to pay. . . . If we didn't, the organization would stop. There were times when the president would give us time to raise the money, but we always had to pay. And, I guess, when you're part of the gang you care for it. So, if you care about the gang , you always find the way to get your hands on some money. It's like, if you care for your girlfriend, you always find a way to make her happy. With the gang you had to find the money to keep it happy.

Money for the centralized fund is secured through other means as well; after all, membership dues contribute only a very limited amount. Included in these activities are stealing and the sale of weapons and car parts. While recalling his early days in the gang, Red describes his working relationship to senior gang members to whom he was assigned: "The older guys would always bring me and tell me to go steal or sell this or that—and that this would bring money for me, but most of the money had to be taken to the box for dues. They would tell me that the money would be used for getting me out of jail or any trouble that I might get into later." Hector gives a similar account: "In our gang we collected dues. Everybody had to pay. Several times I worked hard with other guys pulling some jobs; we stole a car and stripped it. The guy in charge took most of the money for the box because we were empty. I guess we didn't mind that much because it all comes back."

A more indirect mode for generating funds for the box is through contributions made periodically by the supplier. Because the supplier has a vested interest in the survival of the gang, there are times when he uses his own funds for resolving certain gang-related problems. The supplier understands quite well that, without his monetary donation, the gang might suffer a crushing downturn. Similarly, he understands that, without the gang organization, he could lose his business; after all, it depends heavily on the gang's capacity to sustain itself. In most cases, monetary contributions made by the distributor are geared to protecting his workers, his street-level dealers. If and when these workers are apprehended by the police, the distributor puts up the money for getting them out of jail. In the following exchange Carmelo provides a graphic picture of the distributor's role as a protector of the well-being of the organization and its members.

Felix: How often did the distributor use his money to get members out of jail?

Carmelo: Many. We had some times when they pull the money out of their own pockets, and one of us would get bailed out—or sometimes to pay a hospital bill for someone who got really busted up in a fight.

Felix: And why did the distributor do this?

Carmelo: They would do it really out of their own goodwill, for the devotion they have for their own gang. And they want everybody out in the hood; they figure the more of us who are out there, the better for everyone.

Felix: What were the other reasons the distributor used his money to get people out of jail?

Carmelo: One thing you have to understand is that, without the guys, the distributor doesn't have a business. Who does the real business for him and the gang? We do. So, he needs to have his fellas out—out there making him some money.

Felix: Did this happen to you?

Carmelo: Yes, I was taken out several times. One time I got busted along with my two partners, and we walked a few hours later. Our mainhead needed us out there. So, he put up the money real quick.

Felix: You said earlier that one reason the big guys get others out of trouble situations is to demonstrate to everybody else that they are devoted to the gang and that they care for the gang. Elaborate on this.

Carmelo: They want to show everybody in the gang that they are devoting everything they have to the gang to make it better. And to take—how can I say it?—"look what I did for you!" kind of thing. And they tell everybody, "That's why I'm leader, and that's one reason I want all of you to look up to me."

This chapter takes us far beyond the popular view of the youth gang as a highly disorganized collection of psychopaths who are only interested in bringing physical punishment and harm to others. It demonstrates unquestionably that the Diamonds represent a very highly organized, hierarchally arranged business enterprise. The discussion shows, however, that the Diamonds developed into a business enterprise over time. They were not initially formed to deal in drugs. At first, members of the gang used drugs only recreationally. As time passed, the thrust of the organization changed and the Diamonds began operating in the world of drug dealing.

The process leading to the transformation of the youth gang into a business gang was complex. Many factors contributed to the formation of the Diamonds as a business operation, both external forces and internal cultural group dynamics. What emerged was a systematic and highly organized set of business relations among gang members.

Chapter

5

Becoming a Street-level Dealer

Between the gang's two occupational poles of drug distribution and stealing stand street-level cocaine and marijuana dealers. In most cases the same individual performs both jobs, though sometimes the choice is to work only one. Because the price of marijuana is constantly in flux—resulting in erratic and often low profit margins—youngsters dealing at the street level tend to prefer the job of cocaine dealing. Estimating the total number of Diamonds working as street-level cocaine dealers is difficult, but the fact that most of the ones I spoke to indicated a preference for dealing this drug serves as evidence of the perceived profitability of the job. Since members of the Diamonds dealt in both cocaine and marijuana at one time or another, I will simply refer to these workers as street-level dealers without differentiating between one or the other drug.

What can be asserted rather easily is that street-level drug dealing is an occupation that members attain only after having undergone a long, intricate, and, at times, frustrating process. As in more legitimate careers involving newcomers, members of the Diamonds who wish to become dealers must develop the requisite background and skills as well as harmonious relationships with significant persons in the business. (In the case of the

117

Diamonds members have to work on establishing unblemished affiliations with the most influential members of the gang.) Both qualifications are acquired through a sequence of stages. In the discussion that follows, I provide an account of the the steps members of the Diamonds go through to become street-level dealers. I will also point out the various risks and threats facing these young people along the way and the means they use to offset these hazards.

It is important to note that the stages followed by members of the Diamonds in moving from one job to another are highly idealized, and often several alternative processes are at work. In other words, within the Diamonds there is wide divergence from the model outlined below. Some young men, for example, are involved in different jobs at the same: stealing, serving as runners for marijuana and cocaine dealers, stashing guns and stolen goods, and other related activities. Other members remain in a particular job for the entire time of their involvement in the gang.

⚍ Stealing

In chapter 4 I portrayed stealing as one way members of the Diamonds raise money for themselves and the gang. Though the gains from this activity are relatively limited, stealing represents an important step one takes to move up the ranks of the gang.

The job of stealing is usually assigned to the Pee Wees, or Littles, the younger gang members, who are typically thirteen to fifteen years in age. There are several reasons for charging the Pee Wees with the responsibility of carrying out stealing and other similarly hazardous job assignments. First, as newcomers, the Pee Wees are expected to demonstrate their commitment and loyalty to the gang. Stealing is regarded as one task designed specifically for this purpose. Second, gang leaders recognize that the legal justice system is less than efficient when dealing with minors, when these youngsters are apprehended for committing acts that are in direct violation of the law. Third, Pee Wees are perceived by older gang members as "crazies"—youngsters who think and care very little about their actions. Some Pee Wees willingly adopt this identity and, indeed, carry out their activities much in line with the typecast. They believe it is to their advantage to perform in accordance with the gang's expectations, hoping that this form of behavior will be generously rewarded. It is not uncommon to hear, for example, such arguments as: "We can count on Jimmy—he's crazy. He's down for the gang; he will do it. We should take care of Jimmy because he is never scared to do anything for the gang." This is the kind of positive evaluation Pee Wees aspire to. Fourth, there are some individuals within the ranks of the Pee Wees who come to the gang already possessing a background or reputation in stealing. These youngsters do not hesitate to display their talent, believing that it will gain them prestige over others with less experience.

Stealing represents work that is very risky because the potential for discovery is extremely high. Therefore, almost by necessity, stealing becomes a group undertaking. Most stealing activities described to me by members of the Diamonds are said to have been carried out by a group, or crew, of two to five gang members. More dangerous jobs require additional manpower at which time the size of the crew increases. It is rare for an individual to "pull a job" or "score," on his own. In cases when this does occur the gang will not sanction the behavior. In fact, there have been cases when individuals were severely penalized for carrying out thefts on their own. Overall, as shown before, the Diamonds live and die by the fundamental principle of collectivism, which discourages individual action.

The significance of the group approach to stealing can be seen in the following remarks, which also tell a great deal about the repercussions for individuals who decide to work on their own.

Felix: When we were talking earlier about stealing you phrased it in terms of "we were stealing this and that." What did you mean by *we?*

Carmelo: Actually, that's what starts it—the gang. Back then we were called the "Littles," so they would say, "Let's get the Littles to do it." And we would go out as a team and do a job.

Felix: What's a team?

Carmelo: Just a number of guys. Sometimes there were three guys; other times we would go out with eight.

Felix: Why would you need eight guys?

Carmelo: They were our watchdogs. Sometimes people who saw what we were doing would come out and try to intimidate us, but when they see all these other guys they become scared. Besides, the gang would get real upset if they ordered us to do a job and we did it alone. Sometimes we would get a V. A V stands for violation, and, if you get one, you get rolled on by a bunch of guys.

Felix: But why were you given a V for stealing? After all, if you got into trouble, you would have to pay for it yourself.

Carmelo: Well, maybe you're right, but it doesn't work like that in the gang. Because, you see, if guys go on their own and do jobs on their own and make money, then the gang doesn't get no money. Besides, the gang doesn't want people to get greedy.

In addition, the partnership offers a greater probability of accuracy in defining situations and solving problems since groups have a greater number of resources for coming up with ideas and for dealing with circumstances of error than individuals. Hence, as a group, youngsters can better plan and execute a job. Even when an individual member presents a robbery plan to his associates, there is always deliberation about it by crew members before executing the plan. Similarly, the partnership allows for task specialization, necessary for carrying out different robberies and planning strategies. Task specialization is usually determined on the basis of personal work preferences and a related repertoire of skills, which can be adopted to fit various stealing activities should reasons of practicality, economics, and unique opportunities so dictate. It is not uncommon to find a stealing group that includes an individuall whose mechanical prowess is great. Some youngsters, for example, are especially good at breaking into cars. Most members of the Diamonds who have been involved in stealing have developed skills in car burglary.

Rafael's memories of his burglary crew provide us with a clear picture of the dynamics of this type of work association: "I used to work with two of the boys all the time. We came into the gang together, so we knew each other real good. For a while we worked separately, but then we came together, and that was really 'bad.' I think we had the baddest crew in the Diamonds. The thing about our group is that we went after the things we liked and were good for selling. We knew what we wanted to go after. We were car thieves, and my boy Pete—Pete is serving time for something that some other shithead did, but Pete was good. Not once were we ever busted."

"I just remember this one time we were chased, but we knew where to hide. There was this gangway that he [Pete] knew about. So, we ran a few blocks then, and, real quickly, we were gone. We ran through this gangway, then we crossed the alley and then another gangway, and we were at this schoolyard, and there was a park next to the school. There were other fellas playing ball there, so we pretended to be with them. We hung out for a while and then headed to the hood."

"This is why were were good. We always informed one another. We were always on the alert. We knew where to go when things got dangerous and messy. And because of that we were always clean. The law just couldn't catch up with us."

It may be argued that, in terms of the explicit goals of the partnership, this type of arrangement, into a cooperative crew, is functional. Forcing an unwilling or dissident member to join a robberty would only endanger the stealing crew. To diverge from one's line of expertise, however, encourages the hazards implicit in lack of practice and unfamiliarity. Only in unusual circumstances does someone from a crew engage in robberies he dislikes and for which his skills are illsuited.

Pee Wees learn to steal by working together with another gang member who has experience, whose role is that of mentor and leader. In an informal conversation Coco provides insight into this process:

Felix: What do you mean by "turning you on"?

Coco: He [Coco's mentor] was the one who was teaching me the ropes.

Felix: And who was that person?

Coco: My main man.

Felix: What about stealing? How did you learn this?

Coco: From my main man. He would teach me everything. I was under his wing. So, what he knew he was going to teach me.

Felix: Why did he do this?

Coco: He was supposed to. Part of his job was to train the new ones like me. What did we know when we came? Not much. I didn't know too much at this time. There are some people that come in bragging. They want to make everybody believe that they are bad and that they have done jobs before. But everybody knows that they ain't shit. We know who's doing what out in the streets. That's our business—to stay in tune with what's happening. So, these guys . . . all they be is a lot of talk, you know, *mucha mierda* [lots of shit].

Felix: So, what are some of the things you learned from the guy you call your main man?

Coco: Like in stealing autos, he taught me to put the screwdriver on the corner of the window; it pops the window without shattering it—no noise. He taught me how to peel the column. You peel the bottom piece, and the rod is right there. You pull up the shoehorn, and it is straight; you turn on the car; you steer the steering wheel, put the car in drive, and you're gone. That's how he taught me. He would stand by the window of the car telling me "Hurry up—do this and do that."

Felix: He wasn't helping you?

Coco: No, he was watching to see that nobody was coming. He was watching me, too. He had to make sure that I was doing it right.

Felix: And how long did he work with you?

Coco: Well, because I learned fast and good, he kept me. My main man liked me a lot, so that too. We were good friends. I think you have to be to do this kind of work.

Gang members define specific items or goods as attractive for stealing and fencing (passing stolen goods along from one person to another to blur the identity of the actual thief)—for example, cars and their parts and household goods, such as videocassette recorders (VCRs), stereos, TVs, and jewelry. Preference is given to those items with the highest consumer demand. Youngsters steal merchandise they know can be easily sold to permanent customers. Some youngsters usually sell their goods to neighborhood residents who the youngsters know cannot afford to purchase from regular retailers. As indicated by Elf, "We knew that some of the older guys in the neighborhood were in need of a car or parts for a car. So, we would tell them that we could get the parts and all they had to do was to leave their garage door unlocked. We would come, steal the car, and stick it inside the garage. If they only needed a certain part, we would put the car inside the garage, strip it, leave him the parts he needed, and take the rest with us. Sometimes they used to come to us to order whatever they needed."

There were other instances when goods were stolen precisely for use by individuals running "chop shops," legal business operations described by members of the Diamonds as being heavily dependent on stolen goods. I was told many stories about the business of the chop shop; many youngsters indicated knowing of at least one, and most claimed to be aware of many. In the dialogue that follows Coco provides a penetrating account of the nature of the chop shop operation.

Felix: You mentioned the idea of a chop shop. What is that exactly?

Coco: These are legal corporations or businesses that buy stolen merchandise cheap and sell it at a higher price.

Felix: Give me an example.

Coco: We would steal a car and leave it at a certain spot, and they pick it up. They would pay us in advance, and they would come with tow trucks and drive it away.

Felix: A certain spot, like what?

Coco: Well, like a street. We would drive the car to the street they tell us and leave it there, go to them, they give you the money, and you tell them where it is, and they come and pick it up. They take all the parts themselves. All the parts' serial numbers are changed, and the parts become ready for sale.

Felix: So, a chop shop is a legal business?

Coco: Yes, it could be an auto body shop, auto parts, a mechanic's garage—they might need certain things to sell to their customers. So, they come to us and tell us to get them this or that part. We get them the part, and they put their own serial number on it, and that makes it legal. Like stolen radios, you can take them to an electronics shop, and they include them with their stock, and it can't never be proven that it's stolen because it is part of their stock, and it has a legal serial number. We call this a tag job.

Felix: Are the chop shops local, like in this neighborhood?

Coco: They are all over the place, not only in this neighborhood but in others. There could be one right here in this community, and nobody knows.

Felix: How do you find them? How do they find you guys?

Coco: They go out and look into what they consider bad neighborhoods, like our neighborhood. This is not a bad neighborhood, but they know that we are here. They got connections. These guys think that because we are gang-bangers that we can do these things for them.

Felix: What do you mean by that?

Coco: Well, that just because we are bangers we are supposed to know how to do this kind of work—that we are good at this because they think that that's we do. Besides, if we get caught, who are we? We're just bangers. If we squeal on them, they know they're safe because the law is not going to take our word.

Felix: So these guys are keeping you guys employed?

Coco: Yes, but it's not legal. This is not the kind of job you want to tell people about. Like, if you go to McDonalds' or wherever to look for a job, you just don't tell them that you had this kind of job. They're going to want to know what kind of experience you have, but this is not a legal gig. So, we don't tell what we do in this line of work. Anyway, these guys are slick. They make the operation seem legal. They come in with their own tow trucks, so the police would think that it's legal; they come in with their own equipment, and nobody knows that they are illegal. Then they stick a number on the stuff and make it legal.

Felix: And what do you think of these guys?

Coco: Hey, man, like, they have to survive. This is survival out here. They are beating the law. That's what everybody learns.

Felix: Would you do something like that if you were in the same position as these guys?

Coco: I don't know. That's dangerous. If I had my own business, I would try to stay clean.

Another major skill young members of the Diamonds must learn during this stage of burglary work is locating and selecting potential "scores." That is, they need to learn of places in which they can secure the merchandise they are involved in peddling. According to members of the Diamonds, they do not burglarize in their own neighborhood. There is, in fact, a gang policy that serves to discourage youngsters from including neighborhood residents and their property as part of their stealing pool. As stated by several members of the Diamonds, the view shared by most youngsters is that they need to keep the neighborhood fairly stable and peaceful to ensure that their drug operations run smoothly and to prevent their parents from discovering that they are affiliated with the gang.

For these reasons thefts and burglaries committed in Suburbia are often blamed on local neighborhood youth not associated with gangs. Tony explains: "I know the two guys who are terrorizing the hood. These two guys are stoned thieves. But, since they look like everybody, you know, like other teenagers or like regular bangers, people think it's us. But these guys don't belong to a gang. They are not Diamonds. They are some of these neutrons that sometimes try to make trouble for us. But you know what? Anything that happens here is blamed on us. When things are stolen around here, when things are missing, do you know who is fingered? Us! What some people don't understand is that we have respect for where we live. Our guys don't steal around here. We want our neighborhood clean and without trouble. We got enough trouble as it is. But you know what is interesting about these two guys? Well, I'll tell you. They could go loose. The police could come after us and forget about the people who are really going around giving people a hard time and taking their things."

Carmelo adds, "You really have to be stupid to steal in your own neighborhood. Come on, now—we are not that damn stupid. If you want people coming after you, then go and take their shit. Once you steal in your neighborhood, forget it—people will find you, and they try getting on your case. Who wants that? And, you know, where can we go if we mess with the people here? Besides, if you take their stuff, where are you going to sell it? I just think that people should know that we are a little smarter than what they think. That's just too stupid to do. Maybe other gangs do it that way. But around here we have respect."

It is also believed that members from rival gangs deliberately burglarize local neighborhood residents for the purpose of upsetting relations between the Diamonds and their neighbors. Coco elaborated on this perception: "There are guys from enemy gangs who are sent out to our hood to give people a hard time and even to steal from them. What they want to do is to put us in a bad situation with the people around here so the people can turn against us. When we find out that this is happening we play the same game, too. We call this a risk game."

"There was this one time that one of the neighbors that we know, and they know us too, told us that they had seen a guy breaking into the house next door. They told us what the dude looked like, and we knew that he was not with us. So, the chief got really pissed off and told us to go and do a number in the hood of [the opposition gang]. So, I went with my main man and this other guy and ransacked this apartment. We went and took some shit from there. It was nothing important, but we turned the apartment inside out. And you know why we did this shit? Because they did it to us."

Because of their commitment to maintaining Suburbia in a state of serenity, members of the Diamonds who steal must develop appropriate methods for locating potential scores outside of their neighborhood. One of the most regularly employed approaches involves traveling by car in search of areas in the city which seem to contain desired goods, principally car models youngsters believe will "bring the most amount of cash." On these "scouting trips" youngsters are accompanied by an older and experienced member who has knowledge of these neigborhoods. During these early trips youngsters are shown a neighborhood with potential, its apparent dangerous spots (that is, places to avoid), and the different car models desired. Carmelo recalls going out on his first "expedition" and the knowledge he gained from it. "We didn't steal anything the first time we went. This guy wanted to show me the neighborhood and the things he thought I needed to learn. We drove around, and then he took me over to a street. We got out of the car and walked half a block. He took me behind one car and said, 'Look, if we are going to steal this car, you can see from here how dangerous it is. This street is not protected. Anywhere in this street people can see us.' So, I learned not to mess in places like that. I'm sure that, if I was by myself that day, I would have gotten caught because there were some Saabs and Toyotas, and, you know, the cars we are after—but [places] that are usually patrolled."

Another major source of information that youngsters use for locating potential scores are the customers themselves. Chop shop operators and regular customers provide youngsters with tips about merchandise they want and its location. Coco describes an ongoing relationship he has established with one chop shop operator, who frequently visits him to request certain merchandise and provides him with information about where to obtain it: "This guy started trusting me. He knew I needed the cash and I wasn't going to rat, and, besides, nobody believes a gang member. Anyway, he would tell me of specific places where I could find this or that. He was as much a thief as I was. My biggest score with this guy was a Mazda car. He described the kind of car he wanted and told me of several places to go. One was by the ballpark—you know, where the Cubs play. I drove by there with my main man. This was very dangerous because this was the hood of an opposition gang. So, we had to be really on the alert. We found a car on Wayne Street. It was blue, and we brought it back to where he was going to pick it up."

Elf recounts a similar experience: "Without the tips from this guy who owned [the electronics] shop I never would had learned of [that area]. He knew the different places there real good. He knew houses and apartments where I could go for VCRs and stereos. I only did it several times because the other guys thought that he was a narc and was setting us up. So, we stopped. And I wasn't sure about this guy. Everybody was suspicious."

While the act of stealing is dangerous, risky, and requires much preparation and planning, sales of stolen goods usually produce small earnings for these youngsters. In the following account Tito provides a brief description of the monetary payoff of stealing: "We stole this one car because it had some little seats a guy in the neighborhood needed. And, so, we went and took the car, and this car had a nice radio, and I took the radio and sold it, and that's how we used to keep money in our pockets so we could get new gym shoes and things like that. What was I making? Sometimes I pocketed fifty [dollars]. Sometimes my take was twenty. You know, enough to get me by." In a similar way Lobo describes making only enough money to take his girlfriend to the movies and, at times, out for dinner: "I never made a lot of money through stealing. Most of the money I got I used it for being with my girlfriend. We would go to get a bite and then to the show. Sometimes we did it the opposite way, but always I spent the money quick and on her."

From the descriptions provided above by Lobo and Tito as well as those by other youngsters it is not difficult to discern the "profit-sharing" dimension of group theft. Simply put, youngsters are expected to share equally with their partners whatever they make from stolen goods. According to Coco, "We were making spending money—only enough to buy little things. So, why not split the money three ways or four ways? I always liked working with my partner, and sometimes we brought one other guy with us, so it was a three-way split. We knew that we were not going to get rich from one job, so what we made was split between the three of us. And it didn't matter what I did or the other guy did; I never took more than what we gave him. That was our policy— even sharing."

When the job of stealing produces negative results it is expected that the entire working crew absorbs the blame. That is, as partners, members of the Diamonds not only share the profits but also any losses from stealing. Elf provides a vivid description of this element of sharing while recounting one incident that led to the apprehension of his entire crew: "We went to get this car for a chop shop deal, and after we got it we decided to drive around for a while. It was a new Toyota—you know, one of those Camrys that . . . they have everything. So, we were cruising through the north side, trying it out. Hell, we decided to have some fun with the car before giving it up. But then the law spotted us, and they started chasing us. And I was with my boys; there were three of us. I was driving, so I took the car through alleys and shit, but they got us because I got into one alley that was blocked by a garbage truck. So, we closed the windows of the car, and the police came, and we refused to open the windows or the doors. Then I said to the guys that it was cool, that I was going to open up but that nobody say nothing. So, we walked out, and the cops proceeded to search us and the car, and then they started punching us and beating all three of us. But we didn't talk. We all said that someone else gave us the car to take someplace. We stuck to that story. We all got busted together. That's how it is with us; we do it together, and we pay together."

In effect, the major outcome of stealing is seldom measured by economic benefit but, rather, by the sense of achievement experienced by youngsters who manage the operation successfully and use their mechanical expertise. A "beautiful job" does not necessarily indicate that a large amount of money was taken or made; it also suggests an appreciation of a crew's craftsmanship. In this way, the youngster working in stealing operations resembles the craftsman whose reward is more psychological than economic.

Additionally, it is more appropriate to speak of gang members involved in stealing—in particular, the Pee Wees or Littles—as "career thieves" rather than "professional thieves": They view stealing strictly as a stage in their participation in the life of the gang and not as a permanent business. Through acts of stealing these newer gang members demonstrate "how much heart they have" and the skills they have learned and can offer to the gang—all of which are essential ingredients for measuring the kind of recognition and acceptance bestowed upon an individual member. (Pee Wees make a distinction between the "skilled" and "inept" thief. In most cases this contrast has to do with one's orientation toward law enforcement. To be a skilled thief is to have developed skills that minimize one's chances of being apprehended. The gang responds quite favorably to those youngsters possessing this special competence.) Thus, the major significance of stealing stems from its symbolism as an expression of fidelity and an act of commitment to the virtues of the gang. Consider the following explanation taken from an interview with Rafael, who reached the level of cocaine dealer: "In gangs there are members that are different in their own way. You might have the quiet type of guy; you might have the real wild one that likes to steal; you might have another that likes to do drugs; you might have all different types of characters. But there is one thing if you want to advance and show that you're bad and that you're real cool and that the gang could trust you selling drugs—if that's what you want, then you must prove yourself by stealing, by writing on the walls of another gang and showing that you're not a snitch."

═ *Marijuana and Cocaine Dealers*

Youngsters who win the support of leaders and older members of the gang and have performed skillfully in various stealing projects become part of the pool of workers who are considered for jobs in marijuana and cocaine dealing. It is important to remember that these gang members are quite young, ranging in age from fifteen to eighteen years; their youthfulness is combined, therefore, with a lack of financial resources. The "post-stealing stage" thus occurs within the context of continual labor dependency and domination. Street-level dealers are not independent workers; rather, they are employed by the gang's distributors, or mainheads, and perform their jobs in accordance with job rules established by their superiors.

For street-level dealers working for "the man," as they tend to refer to their distributor, is regarded as an obligatory stage for raising the necessary financial capital with which to eventually loosen this relationship of dependency and domination. Their ultimate goal is to establish a business operation, to become independent entrepreneurs in order to have direct control over their work and lives. Youngsters enter street-level dealing occupations with the expectation that, if they learn to become ingenious and proficient salesmen during this stage in their drug-dealing careers, they will be able to amass the amount of money necessary to reduce their dependence.

But what really happens to these youngsters? What are the different jobs these youngsters must perform before achieving the position of independent businessmen? What are the aptitudes required for succeeding in these different jobs? How do the youngsters learn and develop these abilities?

Runners

In the majority of cases youngsters who go into marijuana and cocaine dealing begin by working as "runners," or "mules," for distributors within the gang. The runner's major job responsibility is making deliveries, or "drops," of merchandise to customers. Sometimes a runner is responsible for collecting money from customers as well. Rafael, who started running for a distributor at the age of fourteen and became a dealer a couple of years later, recalls that his early job as a runner entailed dropping off merchandise several times a week to different places in the city.

He says, "I was just like a runner. I never bought or had enormous quantities, and I never cut it up myself. No, I never got that far into it then. That happened later, much later. But I was running for a year. I did it for a year. I did it for this big-time dealer in our gang. He was trying me out at the time 'cause he liked me a lot; we worked together. He was older, and he knew I was very streetwise. I knew the neighborhood. So, he needed someone he could trust. Since I was young and dumb-witted . . . he knew that. So, he gave it to me. He would give me, like, fifteen little quarters [quarter ounces] and fifty-dollar bags, and I would drop it at their houses."

To be a runner a member of the Diamonds is supposed to demonstrate that he is tough and can be trusted. Additionally, he is expected to show a sincere ambition to work his way up in the gang. Tony defines himself as someone who has always been "good for the stuff" he was running, or muling. He defines being good as being someone who is willing to fight to protect the merchandise he has been trusted with. "My chief always said that he didn't want chumps handling his merchandise," recalls Tony. "He liked guys who didn't take shit from nobody, who were always willing to protect his stuff. I can understand that. If I was a mainhead, I'd have to know who my runners are. There has to be some trust. I have to make sure that they are going to carry the mission without taking the shit people sometimes gave me when I was running. Then there are guys who are punk: They let other people take their shit. That won't work with me. I got to trust the cat with my merchandise. I got to know who he is. I won't hire just anyone. He's got to be known and respected by others and by me."

In addition, youngsters working as runners understand this line of work to be irregular and temporary. Runners are aware that their job is activated when a customer requests that his purchased goods be delivered or when it is highly risky for the distributor himself to pick up the merchandise. Once again Rafael describes his experiences with running, a job that offered him only occasional employment: "What I didn't like about running was that sometimes I didn't work for weeks, especially when things got hot and we had to chill out for a while. There wasn't much work coming my way. I used to become anxious. I wanted to get on with the work."

Coco's job as a runner was so sporadic that he continued stealing cars to supplement his income. He recalls: "At first you think that you are done with all your car breaking and stuff like that. You do this shit work for a while, and then you think it is over—that you're never going to break into another car. That is complete bullshit. You find out, like it happened to me, that you work when your mainhead wants you to. If there is nothing to deliver, you're really fucked. You're out of luck, buddy, because you don't work. You don't make no money. And all the mainhead says is that something is going to turn up soon. But it never does. So, I told my main man that I wanted to stay with his crew going after cars and shit. And, like I told you before, he liked me, he liked my work, so he said, 'Sure, come on over.' And I did. What do you expect people to do when they can't make money?"

A significant thing about running is that it provides youngsters with opportunities to develop good business skills. Some feel that the most important skill they learned during this stage was how to manage people. Youngsters note the importance of learning how to handle their customers, not letting them take advantage of the youngsters' youthfulness and inexperience. Rafael states, "I learned to be very cautious because I was delivering stuff for some people, and, since I was so young, they could just take it from me. This is something the mainhead said to us. He told us all the time to be cool, to protect his shit. I knew that we had to. So, I knew that I did not want to be violated because I was stupid and let some fuckhead take my shit. So, since I did not want to be ripped off, I did like my mainhead said. I learned to guard myself. I always tried to show the clients that I was in control."

Elf recalls a specific incident that shows how vulnerable the runner is and the importance of learning to manipulate customers. "One time this guy did not want to pay me. I was supposed to collect the money from him, and he had done the same to one of the fellas. This was news with us. Everybody knew that this guy . . . that he could not be trusted. So, I left the stuff hiding and went to him and asked to see the money. Then I asked him for the money. When he gave it to me I gave him the shit."

Through the runner's job youngsters learned quickly about labor exploitation—in particular, about the abundant financial advantages enjoyed by the distributor because of their work. Young men running for distributors come to the fast realization that this type of work always benefits the distributor. At the same time they learn that the wages they are paid will always be meager. While the inequities affixed to the job of stealing were at best glossed over by youngsters—they accepted them as necessary for meeting certain expectations by older members, or, as the youngsters put it, "for proving themselves"—conditions of work injustice found in running are viewed through different lenses: Youngsters simply refuse to accept unfair circumstances.

Yet, it is interesting to observe the response given by runners to conditions of work domination. At this stage they remain faithful to the gang's mainheads and do not blame them for the shortcomings of the running job. They do not always recognize the various forms of manipulation used by distributors to keep them dependent and part of an exploited labor force. They are unaware that runners represent an "army of reserve workers" used by the mainheads to keep the street-level dealers in conditions of subordination.

Instead, runners share the view that the intrinsic nature of their occupation is chiefly responsible for producing such limited wages. As Tony puts it, "The problems with running as we saw it was that there was not enough of it. Our chief would always be saying that people were not buying, that people were not using as much, that people were buying larger quantities and then they would chill out for a while. So, for us that meant that we could only make a drop once in a while. That's how things were. We couldn't change that."

As a result, most of the youngsters maintained that this form of labor exploitation could be best resolved once they had achieved the occupation of street-level dealer. They developed the view that, as permanent street-level dealers, they could accumulate real gains, enabling them finally to realize the dream of the independent distributor.

Thus, in a paradoxical way the job of running, or muling, provides youngsters with opportunities to develop some valuable business smarts as well as alerting them to their subordinate position within the business structure of the gang. Members of the Diamonds working as runners become cognizant of the fact that everyone is not equal within the ranks of the organization and that those individuals employed by the mainheads as runners are often the most exploited. Aware of this form of manipulation, youngsters seek to improve their conditions by becoming street-level dealers.

Street-level Dealers

Street-level dealing is the job into which runners move. Most of the youngsters become "hired dealers," working for the distributor on a consignment basis—that is, they receive on credit, or are fronted, an amount of marijuana and/or cocaine they are responsible for selling and paying the distributor. Youngsters working as hired dealers are those who have demonstrated a convincing measure of work knowledge and loyalty to the distributor—the ones who have performed their running assignments satisfactorily and with the fewest squabbles. In other words, hired dealers represent a group of youngsters who have won the respect of the distributor and can be trusted with a fairly large amount of merchandise, which they now become responsible for selling on the streets.

In his earliest memories as a hired dealer Rafael recalls the reasons why he was selected to work for his distributor: "I was down for the mainhead and the gang—that's why he trusted me. There were some guys who were running who really fucked up. You know, one lost a large quantity of drugs to some punks on the way to a delivery. There was another fuck-up who got busted by the law a couple of times. Hey, who wants them? This was a business. I was cool. I did real good. So, the mainhead asked me to work for him. I showed him that I knew the hood, the people. I was cool."

The job of hired dealer is the most readily available within the ranks of the gang's occupational structure. It is to the advantage of the distributor to have as many youngsters dealing for him as possible. So, while the distributor must take great care to select youngsters who are trustworthy, he must also maintain a large work force working at all times. Tony provides an insightful explanation for this arrangement. We were hanging out one day on the street directly opposite several youngsters who were at work. Recognizing the arrival of a mainhead onto the scene, he commented: "You know, the mainheads don't work the streets. Every once in a while you see them; they want to make sure that their guys are straight and doing their jobs. Like today, this dude is here, but after that you don't hear from him or see him again for a long time. I think that the last time I saw this guy was, like, a couple of weeks ago. The mainheads like to live off of other people. But what happens with the mainheads is that they have to hire some of these guys to deal. They are not going to do the work themselves, so they hire some of the guys and hope for the best. But, you know, that's how business is. How do you know how people are going to work out? You give them a chance, keep them under your control as much as possible, and make sure that they make a little money for themselves so they won't get too uptight." In view of what Tony had just said I asked him to describe the way he would carry out his business relations with street-level dealers if he were to ever become a distributor. He indicated that he would do what others had done: "Why change it if it works? I mean, it seems to me that the mainheads are doing quite well for themselves. Yes, I want my crew, and I would need to control them. That's just how it is."

Marijuana is the drug most easily sold by hired dealers. Dealers indicate that its common use and popularity are correlated with customers' perception of it as being a relatively mild, pleasurable, and easily managed drug. While cocaine is perceived as addictive and expensive, street-level dealers know that marijuana highs last only a few hours, with no aftereffects, such as hangovers. Flaco explains the high regard clients have for the drug he sells normally: "People have the opinion that cocaine is dangerous. And marijuana, you just smoke it—it's like smoking a cigarette—you just smoke it and get high, and that's it. There's not a real big effect on you; you don't get addicted to it. You know, some people do, but they . . . it's controllable. . . . It's not as bad as cocaine . . . you get hooked. . . . You know, you get rid of marijuana fast. Marijuana goes better than cocaine." He adds "The only bad thing is that reefers leave you with a bad smell—you know what I'm talking about. Cocaine doesn't have a smell. So, with reefer you got to put up with the smell. It tells people that you've been smoking. But to me that was no big deal because everybody smokes, so you smell just like everybody else smells."

Youngsters also believe that the legal penalties for dealing marijuana are less severe than for dealing cocaine, which suggests another explanation for the popularity of marijuana sales. As the dealer sees it, there is no significant enforcement apparatus and no cases of severe punishment of possessors of marijuana. One day while Flaco and I were hanging out and talking by the Diamonds's turf we observed a police bust of a couple of dealers who were selling reefer. The youngsters were forced into the back seat of a policeman's car. After a brief period of interrogation they were released. I asked Flaco to tell me what was going on, and he said, "We sell marijuana to make the money we need in order to buy cocaine. Once you got the cocaine you got the power to bring the money in, but you gotta be careful. You gotta be careful because, if the law catches you selling cocaine, you're in for a long time. The charge is twice as hard as if you were caught selling marijuana. I have gotten busted several times for selling marijuana, but I came back to the streets overnight or in a couple of days. The longest I stayed in was the weekend, and that's because they got me on a Friday. But I know one guy who was grabbed by the law for selling coke; he was in for a long time—I think it was something like six months. And you know we learned from that. We got scared, so we decided not to touch the shit. Most of us stick to reefer. And that's what those guy were selling. They showed me their stuff this morning. They had a couple of bags. They are not going to get locked up for that. The police always tells us that they are not going to waste time preparing all kinds of paperwork so that we could be out on the streets in a couple of hours. So, they throw us inside their car and threaten us. They tell us shit like, 'If I ever catch you with this shit, I'm going to beat the shit out of you,' or 'Maybe we could find other drugs, and then we can really make a case.' But for reefer we walk."

There were a few youngsters within the Diamonds who do manage to go out on their own and become "independent dealers," purchasing merchandise from the distributor in fairly large quantities to generate their own profits but continuing to sell it themselves from the street level. As independents, these youngsters know very well that the return on their investment and labor will always be higher than for the hired dealers, for they are given bargain prices for purchasing large amounts of drugs; plus, they can determine which drugs to sale as well as the number of hours to work. One youngster was very specific in illustrating the profitability of the independent dealership:

Felix: How long did you deal drugs?

Gustavo: Actually, I'm still doing it to this day.

Felix: What was your biggest profit when you were working for the man?

Gustavo: My biggest profit a week was about one-hundred to two-hundred dollars a week. The profit I was making for the guy was sometimes one thousand dollars. Sometimes I would bring him two thousand dollars.

Felix: So you were making very little money.

Gustavo: That's right. He was making all the money. There were Saturdays when I would be counting the money that I was going to take him, and there were times when on a Saturday he would make two thousand dollars.

Felix: Now that you're on your own how much money do you make?

Gustavo: It varies. If I go and buy eight hundred dollars worth of cocaine I can make sixteen hundred dollars—a 100 percent profit. If I package the stuff myself into quarter [quarter ounce] bags, I can make more. Any profit to me is good. I don't have that kind of money, so I buy in smaller quantities.

Felix: What has been the most you've ever made?

Gustavo: I bought four hundred dollars [worth] and took out that plus another four hundred dollars. And I sold that on a Wednesday, Thursday, and Friday.

Another youngster became an independent by putting in long hours in his previous job as a hired dealer.

Felix: How long did you work for the distributor?

Carmelo: For about a year. Maybe a little bit longer.

Felix: And what kind of money did you make?

Carmelo: I was making peanuts. This guy was paying me about two hundred dollars, and I was returning him two thousand dollars. Can you imagine that? There were weekends when I would bring him two grand, and I kept a couple of bills. Hey, that's when I said to myself, "It's time to go."

Felix: So, what did you do?

Carmelo: There wasn't much that I could do. I stayed working. But the guy got hungry, and he started giving me stuff to sell during the week. I decided that I was going to be out there long enough so I could get the hell out of there.

Felix: How long did you work for the mainhead after this?

Carmelo: I stayed for a while, over a year.

Felix: Why so long?

Carmelo: You need quite a bit of money to buy your own stuff—I would say about five thousand dollars. You need that much to buy the amount of stuff that can make some money. I never made this much, but I made enough to buy the stuff myself. I was working for me—for nobody but me.

Felix: What does five thousand dollars buy you in terms of real drugs?

Carmelo: A lot. You can buy enough to make yourself a good profit.

Felix: How long would it take you to get rid of this amount of drugs?

Carmelo: No time. We move that stuff fast. Maybe a week. If we don't move it that fast, then we are not doing a good job. The guys work hard and long hours when they know that there is stuff that needs to be sold, to be moved.

Establishment of a Turf

To be successful in street-level dealing both hired and independent dealers must undergo a process through which they learn major skills and specific strategies for guarding against potential predators. Location of a permanent and stable place from which to sell one's products represents a leading requirement. Rather than securing the kinds of physical facilities used for running conventional businesses, members of the Diamonds, as well as other street-level drug dealers, identify and make claim to an open site in their neighborhood. Usually, the location is a street block or corner, referred to by the youngsters as the turf or marketplace. It is little wonder that much intergang rivalry, fighting and killing stem directly from conflict over control of a neighborhood, which represents the cornerstone of the drug business operations for street-level dealers. A gang possessing a successful turf runs the constant risk of invasion and takeover by others with less productive sites.

The phrase "control of the neighborhood" stands for gang ownership of territory from which to conduct business activities. Running a business from a neighborhood street or corner provides youngsters with several money-saving opportunities: They are not required to invest in the acquisition of a business license or insurance, nor are they compelled to pay rental and utility expenses. Some gangs, however, choose to run their business from an apartment.

Membership in a gang aids in the acquisition of a turf, as the gang provides its street-level dealers with accessibility to the sites in the neighborhood it already controls. Many of the Diamonds's street-level dealers inherited the turf that was established by an earlier generation of members. Flaco is quick to point out his good fortune for having taken over a turf with an eminent history: "When I started we already had our corner. This is a famous corner, a popular corner; people know about us. We get all kinds of customers. Our job was to keep the other gangs away from our turf. And since this turf is so popular we are going to make sure to keep it forever." In a similar vein Elf says, "Our turf was here when I came. I don't have to worry because people know where to find us. I think that everybody in the city knows that [in this corner] they can find some real good stuff. Our hood has that kind of reputation."

For others control of a turf where sales of marijuana and cocaine could take place resulted from the encroachment of other neighborhoods. In most cases physical violence was utilized for seizing the neighborhood from opposition gangs or establishing a claim on unclaimed territory. Tito recalls weathering a struggle with an opposition gang over one particular territory: "Most of the turfs that we got so far we took ourselves, and nobody has done nothing, or fight us for it. Over at [the school], that turf, that used to belong to [this one gang] and before that to [another gang]. But the [gang] broke up, and we took it. We had fought [a gang] for a long time over this turf. We broke [them] up, and there was no more of them. So, we claimed it; our section got half of the turf."

On a day in early April 1990 Flaco brought to my attention how the Diamonds had ordered several new *puntos*, or markets, to be opened in the neighborhood in reaction to rumors that the police were preparing to shut down their historic turf. Leaders of the organization recommended that those street corners and blocks not belonging to other gangs be taken over. They decided to identify open sites and to station dealers there in order to begin furnishing the area with a business character as well as alerting prospective customers to the existence of the new sites. Flaco said, "We had a meeting last night. The chiefs of our section told us that they were planning to start new gigs in other areas, that we needed to open up new turfs, because the police was going to try to close us down. We don't want to lose our customers, so they want us to start right away. Besides, we have to keep up with the police. When they try to move on us we are always prepared to take action. So, now we are going to beat them in their own game. When they come they're not going to find us here dealing; we're going to be at different *puntos*."

According to members of the Diamonds, there are two leading locations in which street-level dealing is conducted from the turf: from a sheltered apartment, called a "rock house," and the visible street block or corner. "The rock houses around here," explains Lobo, "may have a couple of guys living there or several of them guys, but pretty much they just have like a sofa, TV, and a box [radio, tape, and record player], but other than that they might not even have electricity in the house, gas, or anything. Their sole purpose is to sell. They would make all kinds of entrances, and most of the business is done through the back."

In the brief interchange that follows Elf provides a similar description of the rock house.

Felix: What are rock houses?
Elf: Rock houses are like any apartment building or your own

house that sells drugs—it's a drug house. And it's a place where drugs are sold and parties are thrown sometimes. Most of the time the parties are thrown so you can make a lot of money.

Felix: So, a rock house could be anybody's house or apartment?

Elf: It could even be a garage that they got open, that the law don't know about. There are garages where people are working in, and that's where they sell their stuff.

Members of the Diamonds demonstrate a preference for the street block or corner over rock houses. Youngsters expressed uneasiness about the risk of entrapment associated with the rock house operations, defining them as easy targets for the police. In general, the rock house appears a risky base to members of the Diamonds because it represents a setting over which they believe they have little control. Different forms of surveillance can be used to prevent busts (for example, positioning guards at several places in the rock house), yet there is always the danger of police raids. When such action is employed persons inside the house do not have a way of escaping.

The turf, on the other hand, is part of the street environment youngsters have well under control. That is, these young people believe they possess the essential understanding and knowledge for maneuvering on the streets and managing the various activities taking place there. Youngsters are aware of the many hideouts in the neighborhood, of the places that can provide them with protection against the police. Listen to the way Lobo describes his knowledge of the streets:

Felix: It seems that dealing from the corner is very dangerous.

Lobo: Oh, I agree, but the corner is only one part of the hood.

Felix: Do you mean there are other corners?

Lobo: There is the entire neighborhood. This is our neighborhood. Most of the guys grew up here. We know it. There are people living here who do not know the places we know.

Felix: Which places?

Lobo: Places we use for stashing our stuff, for hiding when we see the law. There's not a place that we don't know about.

Additionally, since drug transactions, like other illegal business exchanges, must be conducted in the shortest possible period of time, the open street markets help to save time. The street block or corner offers high visibility to customers, informing them of the dealer's presence and, in doing so, preventing customers from having to waste time "shopping around." In short, the openness of "street shopping" allows customers to locate promptly the setting in the neighborhood where drugs are available. Working from the street also facilitates open communication between sellers and customers about the brand and price of available drugs. As Elf explains, "We cannot afford losing customers because they can't find us. As long as we are out there, they can't miss us." Likewise, Rafael says, "The one thing about the streets is that I can make my sales quickly. People see me; I come up to them, or they come up to me, and they know what I got. I tell them what's happening, the shit I got and price. And we do it. Hey, that's how you do business—you do it fast." And in the following exchange Flaco provides further evidence of the youngsters' preference for selling from the streets rather than the rock houses.

Felix: When you were dealing drugs why did you do it from a corner or from the middle of the block?

Flaco: Well, there's not really a place to go to sell. Some gangs got rock houses and stuff like that, but I took it in the streets because that's a gold mine—because customers know we are out there. They go there automatically. All you gotta do is put your stuff away, stay out there, make sure the law's not watching.

Felix: What makes the corner a gold mine?

Flaco: I guess people standing out there or people passing by, from friends that they know—they go to their friends and tell them, "We was partying, and it was good stuff." So, they tell their friends where they got the stuff from, and these new customers come by and buy the stuff from us.

Felix: But customers can also go to the rock houses for good stuff. What's the problem with the rock houses?

Flaco: People come who know you—they want credit—they come and say, "You got some, man. I ain't got no money. Can I have some on credit?" And you tell them, "No, man, you can't." They get pissed off and maybe call the law and tell them, "I know where they got a rock house. They got a lot of stuff in there, man." It's not worth it unless you keep it real quiet.

Felilx: How can you do that?

Flaco: The only way you keep a rock house quiet is if you keep two or three of the fellas outside, and they know the customers, and they go and get the stuff themselves.

Felix: So, don't allow the customers into the rock house?
Flaco: Right. Don't show them where it's at. Obviously, they almost always find out.

Safe School Zone

The enactment of state legislation in 1986 called the Safe School Zone contributed directly to making the neighborhood streets the central location for drug-dealing operations. The law was part of a Comprehensive Crime Control Act, which was passed with the aim of curbing drug dealing and use in school buildings and their surroundings. It provided tougher sentences for persons convicted of selling controlled substances within one-thousand feet of a school. Those convicted would face a maximum sentence of thirty years in prison and a $250,000 fine.

As a result of this law, schools, which for a long time had served as profitable markets for drug dealers, were now off limits. Youngsters were forced to take their business to other locations, mainly to the local neighborhood where street blocks and corners were already congested with drug dealing. The enactment of the law also had the indirect result of preventing some youngsters from attending school; after all, they now needed to spend their time away from school competing for the drug market. Overall, though the Safe School Zone legislation forced drug dealing and use out of the schools, it did not stop youngsters from dealing.

Coco was one dealer who had done a good deal of his business in his school building until this legislation was enacted. He says, "My only liking of school was the girls and the money I was making from selling. I dealt there for over a year. I had steady customers. These guys were white, black, Latino, you name it. When it came to drugs we were all on the same team. The gang-banging was put aside because we all had one thing in common—drugs. I banked, and they abused [I sold, and they used]. But then the word got out that I needed to stop dealing in the school because of a new law that said that, if we got caught with drugs inside or near the school, we would be put away for a long time. Before this law I got busted one time by a security guard over at the school, but they let me go because I was a minor. But after this new law it didn't matter your age or whatever; what really counted was whether you were doing it inside the school or outside by the school building. So, I was ordered by my chief to go into the neighborhood and work with some other people over by our turf. And that's what I did. I wasn't going to jail because of some stupid law. So, in the hood we had all these people selling, so we had to share the customers, but that was OK, too, because it was safe there. We were selling there anyway—like, after school and during the weekends. But now we were in the hood all the time. That became like a full-time job."

Several public observances were organized immediately after the enactment of the Safe School Zone to celebrate its passage. Public meetings were held, and a major radio station devoted an entire program one evening to a discussion on the act. Citywide and local community newspapers also participated in the celebration, publishing articles and reports on the law and its implications for school. It was anticipated that schools would become drug-free now that dealers and pushers would be removed from the vicinity, and schools could finally get on with the business of educating students.

It is difficult to measure the academic consequences of the enactment of the law, yet it is clear that large amounts of drugs are still finding their way into schools. Further, neighborhoods located near schools have become extremely crowded with drug-dealing activities. In short, teenage drug dealing has not disappeared; it has simply been transplanted to a different area.

Establishing a clientele and controling customers. Once the turf is established the next major precondition for becoming a successful dealer is finding customers willing to buy available products. The role of the customer is of utmost significance in terms of the growth of the business, for each smoke [of marijuana] or hit [of cocaine] physiologically and psychologically encourages future consumption. And, as the customer consumes more and more cocaine or marijuana, he or she necessarily becomes an advertiser and, in effect, salesperson for the product and salesman who sells it. The basic idea is to use customers to establish a network of referrals.

Coco recounts how he was led to some of his customers: "My biggest voice was a guy that I sold some stuff to one time on credit. He wasn't from the neighborhood. He was called Tall Willie, and he had been my customer for a year or a little more, and one day he asked me for a hit, and I gave it to him. When he came back to pay me he brought two of his friends. This was the first time he did that. These two guys became my customers, too."

"You need to have customers who can trust you—people

who like your stuff and know that you will be there for them. These guys have friends, and then they tell their friends how things are working with their dealers and stuff, and, if they like it, they start coming around."

Unlike legitimate retailers who use different forms of advertising to let as many people as possible know what they are selling and where, street-level dealers of cocaine and marijuana are secretive, wanting only certain individuals to now of their business. Paradoxically, like other jobs involving direct contact with customers, for street-level dealers customers represent a potential problem. Dealers cannot really anticipate the intentions and authenticity of their customers (that is, they cannot be sure if these are real buyers or people wishing to take their merchandise or if they are working for the police or are police officers themselves). Therefore, it is more accurate to talk about controlling customers rather than just identifying and selling to customers.

It is common for customers to try "ripping off" dealers, particularly in cases when some corners develop a reputation as being "soft." There are other instances in which users have a desperate need for drugs and will attempt to rob dealers. For the Diamonds's street-level dealers joint action has become one leading strategy for dealing with these threats. I cannot recall a single day when I visited the neighborhood and found only one gang member walking the streets. A group of young men was always present. If a Diamond were ever alone, he was usually empty-handed; that is, he was not carrying any merchandise. Flaco explains their practice: "We always work in teams of three or more. There are some people from other gangs that I know that take chances; they sometimes do it by themselves. That doesn't work with us. There are too many people around here watching us, especially those crazies—the dopeys. These guys are all fucked up; they are out of their minds. They'll try anything to get drugs. Hey, I don't want to mess with them. So, the way to deal with them is to have your partners watching while you're working the block."

Another method used by street-level dealers to control their customers is to establish a reliable clientele. Dealers try organizing their business around trusted individuals with whom they share ethnic, cultural, or local ties. For the Diamonds their main customers are friends or individuals referred by friends, though they also sell a great deal of their goods to outsiders, usually white, middle-class individuals.

Felix: Who do you sell to?

Tito: Mostly guys, teenagers—not teenagers but like adult teenagers, like anywhere from seventeen and up. Like, I never like to sell to older people, anyone who looks like an adult.

Felix: What do you do when an adult approaches you for some smoke or cocaine?

Tito: I never sell to them. I just tell them I don't know where it's at, I don't know who has it or nothing like that because they could always be an undercover cop, and they bust you. So I like sticking to my age group.

Felix: Who are these guys that you sell to?

Tito: Mostly guys from the neighborhood or guys who wanna be cool, like the neutrons who want to be cool, and some of the gangbangers. They try to smoke, and they try to impress the guys and say "I want to be cool too," so they buy smokes.

Carmelo describes the arrangements he sometimes makes for accommodating his local customers, procedures inspired by his recognition of the strategic significance of maintaining a reliable local consumer base: "We work out different things. Sometimes I just give them the stuff, and they pay me on Friday. Or they have different kinds of things that they use to trade. Like the other day, I had a guy give me this expensive watch; it was a real nice one. Another left with me his VCR. So, there are different ways that we play. These are good people. They are here; they bring me their business all the time. I know that I can trust them. You know, to survive in the business and to keep your customers happy you have to play fair cards. Who knows? I might need some help from them one of these days."

An additional method for controlling the customers is for dealers to be knowledgeable of and to have practical experience with the product they are selling. Sometimes customers inspect and sample the drug before making a purchase and contest the quality of the product. They often ask that the price be reduced, arguing that the cocaine or marijuana is of inferior quality. Dealers must be in a position to balance these challenges and be able to present the product as "legit." This is usually done not only be relying on their selling skills but also, just as important, by having knowledge of the drug, which they have acquired by using. All the members of the Diamonds I talked to indicated having used marijuana or cocaine, or both, before they started dealing. They define themselves as sporadic rather than heavy users; none of them deal to support this habit. In the following exchange Rafael explains how his business smarts and experience as a user helped to establish himself as a responsible dealer.

Felix: You described yourself as a successful dealer. What made you a successful dealer?
Rafael: My experience.
Felix: Which one?
Rafael: I had experience with the drug. I used to smoke reefer.
Felix: And how important was that?
Rafael: Well, you know, if you're going to sell drugs, you just can't pick up some grass from the ground and put it in a bag and expect to sell it. You might sell it to some idiot who's out there. But you've got to know your stuff.
Felix: What do you mean by that?
Rafael: There is a lot of danger in selling drugs. You got to know how to talk to the person. You've got to know who to talk to and know about the drug you're selling. You've got to know the effect it has, how good the reefer is. You've got to know all of that before you sell it. You can't begin without the knowledge to run it.

A similar account is provided by Carmelo: "See, you learn how to bullshit: That's the main thing on dealing. You've got to know how to talk. You just can't say, 'Here,' no matter how good it is. The guy wants to know what you're selling; you've got to know what you're selling. That's the way I did it. I used to always have a few samples on me. I would come to the customer. I tell him I got those nickel bags. I might be on the corner. He might drive by, or he'll come walking by, and he'll say, 'What have you got for the *cabeza* [the head]?' And we'd come to the side of an alley, a building, and I'd show him the bo; he'd smell it. I know what I'm selling, and, if he doesn't want to take my word on it, I'll let him try a joint, and I would smoke with him. You got to know to smoke and enjoy a *bata* [the smoke]. And you would tell him about the sensation you're feeling. That's how you do it."

Control of the "law."   In addition to learning how to handle their customers, street-level dealers must contend with the ever-present possibility of police detection. Since the volume of drugs sold by street-level dealers is small, the goal is to sell to as many customers as possible. There is a danger of falling victim to a "buy-bust," a practice in which the police make a drug purchase then arrest the seller. Additionally, dealers are aware that the police recruit and hire individuals to serve as informants, and in some cases informants make drug buys under police supervision. In general, members of the Diamonds believe that the police are "out there to get us." They are under the impression that police officers consider them to be above the law, capable of avoiding their pressures, and not respectful of the law, as the officers feel they should be. Thus, they are always anticipating or on guard against aggressive police action. Similarly, youngsters share the view that police officers want to retaliate for previous instances when they were not able to make an arrest or when, after making the arrest, they witnessed dealers beating the charge or being released on bail. Youngsters believe they recognize the intentions of the police, and they rely on several methods to reduce their chances of being apprehended.

Some youngsters in the Diamonds employ the "payoff" as one direct means for dealing with police apprehension. They carry out this practice in spite of periodic crackdowns by law enforcement agencies in Chicago and the police reform movement of recent administrations in the city. In the youngsters' opinions police officers can be bought for the "right amount"; that is, money is capable of defusing the feelings of revenge the police might have for them. Gustavo recalls, for example, the time when he was apprehended by two policemen and was let go after paying them a certain amount of money: "There is a danger involved also. One time I got busted with a lot of stuff. These two cops handcuffed me, took me to this office, and threw me on top of this desk. They asked me all kinds of questions, like who I was selling for and stuff like that. I told them that I found the stuff. At this time one of my friends came in, showed the cops a bunch of money, and asked them if they could talk about that. The cops said yes, and I walked. They let me go. They got about two hundred dollars."

Similarly, it is common to hear youngsters talk about drugs representing a form of payoff. They believe that police officers confiscate drugs for their own use. Some members of the Diamonds share the conviction that certain police officers are more interested in seizing drugs than in making actual arrests. Carlos recalls a time when he was making a buy at a rock house and was surprised by two policemen, who, after much talking, walked the two mainheads present during the business transaction to the back of the apartment, seized a large amount of drugs, and left without arresting anyone. "This was the only time I ever went to a rock house for the stuff," he says. "But, actually, it made it seem like no big deal. Nothing happened to anyone. The cops came in and took the shit they wanted and left." Coco remembers several times when policemen came to his corner with specific intentions to confiscate drugs: "These cops would come to the hood, throw me against the wall several times, beat the shit out of me, and take my stuff and walk away. And then they say, 'The next time we're really going to bust your head.'"

Tony's experiences were similar. He recalls one incident in particular: "I was busted one time. This one guy gave me fifty dollars worth of weed [marijuana] and an eight ball worth of caine, which, depending on where you buy it, can go up to about two hundred dollars. Because I was supposed to go take it, a cop busted me and towed me all the way to the north side and left me there. He took the stuff I had, didn't even leave me a dollar for a bus ride home; he left me all the way down by the north side. And he kept the shit. Cops are a gang themselves. The only difference between them and us is that they have a little piece of metal on their chest that says that they can get away with anything. Because, if you think about it, cops do everything we do, except that they're doing it legally. So they think. They take our stuff and use it, and that's legal. You know, sometimes they need some stuff to plant on some people they are getting ready to bust or someone they're trying to make a case against. So, they come and get the stuff from us. It's cheap when they take it from us. They don't have to pay for it. Besides, we cannot make any claims that cops took our drugs."

Notwithstanding the success of the payoff, street-level dealers are well aware of the limited effectiveness of this strategy; they recognize that police officers cannot always be bribed. Thus, they have other, less direct means of handling the police. The joint action strategy, indicated earlier by youngsters and defined as an important tool for successfully managing their customers, is one such approach. Youngsters carry out their work in crews or teams of several members, which serve as protection against police invasions and assaults. In the same way that youngsters working together try to be alert to possible infractions by customers, they are also on a constant watch for the police. When a police car approaches a call is made which acts as a warning to dealers to take cover or be extra cautious. According to Tony, the most effective way to guard against a possible police bust is "to walk," that is, to stroll from one point on the street block to another: "We don't stand in one place all the time. We move; we walk back and forth around the block. This way we can see the entire street. At other times we disappear for a while. You know, we go into somebody's house to chill out. And when we come back one guy comes out, and he walks up and down to see what's happening."

Flaco describes another method used for protecting dealers against possible police seizure: "Usually, when we see people that look suspicious, like cops, those guys, like we show them the bag, and we're like, 'Come out, man. Step out of the car. Come in the hallway. Smoke a joint.' That way we make sure they aren't a cop because, if an officer comes and he agrees to smoke a joint with us, that's an indictment. He is in violation of the law. He's committing a crime, and he will be charged for it. And a lot of customers like to smoke it right then and there, so for some of these people who look suspicious we want them to smoke it there."

The gang itself represents another indirect means for reducing the insecurity caused by the police. When a member is arrested the gang has the responsibility of arranging the bond. The understanding is that the gang provides assistance to the apprehended member by sharing the expenses of court costs if he is arrested "on business." On several occasions Carmelo's bond was paid by his chief. "I told you before that most of us have gotten locked up all kinds of times," he says. "I've been to the house [jail] myself a couple of times, but I got taken out by the chief. They know what we're doing and how dangerous that is. So they go or send someone to get us. Besides, that's why we pay dues, so when we get taken away by the law people will come and take us out."

Finally, faced with the prospect of being apprehended by the police, street-level dealers limit the amount of drugs they carry or keep. They also have devised ways for stashing the drug, creating secret storage places or hideouts. Tito describes the various places and ways he has developed to keep himself clean: "The streets are easier in case the law comes. It's easier to hide stuff because now they have houses that they deal drugs out of, and there you just sit there, and, if the police come, you have nowhere to go. You have to either get rid of the stuff, flush it down the toilet, and, just when the police come in, you're still gonna get whipped by them and harassed and everything. And they try beating you to get everything out of you. They want to know where the stuff is and what you did with it. But, if you're out on the streets, you can stash your stuff. One thing I do is never to keep anything on you; if a customer wants some stuff, you have the person wait until you go and get it. I keep my stuff in hiding places I make; they are not far from the corner. Sometimes I just dig out a hole behind some bushes or by a tree, you know, and stuff like that. Sometimes I just have someone in a building holding the stuff for me. The police will never see that person. There are so many buildings and apartments—how are they going to know where to go and who has the stuff?"

Learning to deal. Dealing itself represents the last major precondition for becoming a successful street-level dealer. The act of dealing entails much more than simply standing on the corner or middle of the street block and disposing of available drugs. Like stealing, the job of dealing is part of a process through which very specific social interaction skills are learned. Youngsters learn to deal by interacting and observing those who have worked in the occupation for some time. Would-be dealers simply hand out and observe the various techniques employed by veteran dealers. The following two accounts furnished by Tito and Flaco, respectively, provide graphic pictures of this process: "Nobody taught me," says Flaco. "I just watched the guys who are used to it and have dealt it for a while. I used to watch them, how they got rid of it on the corner. They just hang out. Sometimes they stash it; sometimes they hold it. And they just let people know they got it without letting everybody know, without calling it out; they just do little signs to people. And they would let them know, 'Hey, I got this, this, and this. And, if you have a friend, tell him to come around at noon, two o'clock, or at whatever time.'"

Felix: How did you learn to deal drugs?
Flaco: By my sellers, other sellers, seeing them do this and that and asking them how do you do this and that.
Felix: What exactly did they teach you?
Flaco: I would observe them hanging out in the neighborhood with the boys.
Felix: What did you see?
Flaco: I saw them running up to cars with weed. . . . Yeah, OK, pull it over.' Then I see them adding it and giving them a certain amount here, ten dollars or something. I saw how they walk to the cars and how they use different signals to tell people what they got.

Another major rule of dealing that youngsters must learn is to work together as a team, or network. This entails conducting their business operation as a collective unit of three or more sellers at all times, sharing potential clients among themselves. Street-level dealers gather daily on the street corner or block and establish relations as business partners as well as friends. These youngsters become committed to one another, protecting each other and sharing various clients. In short, the team approach to dealing allows sellers to have a fair share of the market.

Felix: When you deal with three guys on the corner, how do you get customers?

Tony: We have a system. We take turns.

Felix: Like what?

Tony: Well, let's say that one guys drives—well, then, that might be for Coco. Then the next guy is for Blanco, and then my customer. We rotate.

Felix: How do you feel about this system?

Tony: It's the only way for all of us to make money. If we don't do it this way, we might have a lot of trouble. People will get greedy and try to control or take over. That's like if another gang tried to take over our hood. Hey, we are against that kind of stuff.

As indicated by Tony, the team approach to dealing also reduces the temptation to become selfish—tendencies these youngsters believe are commonly found in conventional business practices and which, in turn, are responsible for much of the discord existing in traditional business circles. Greed and selfishness are viewed with much disregard and contempt by dealers and other members of the gang. Conversely, distributors tend to regard highly those who are ethical and fair in their working relationships with other dealers and with customers. Through the team approach youngsters also learn the value of honor for making it in the drug-dealing world.

Felix: Tell me about Friday's meeting. You said that one of your friends was demoted and sent to another area. What happened?

Flaco: Yeah, Flash, he was being greedy, selling drugs by himself and that, and he would come out on Fridays and Saturdays because he knew those were the days he'd make more money selling drugs, because that's when people get their paychecks. It's mostly the workers that come because, you'd be surprised, because these people that don't got jobs, they don't come. But the people that got jobs come all the time on Fridays and Saturdays. And, anyway, he always comes around on them days, and then on Mondays through Thursdays and Sundays he disappears to la la land, and then he just be using the neighborhood and the guys.

Felix: So, what happened?

Flaco: We told him, and he said he didn't know what we were talking about, and we said that he needed to go to another turf and develop it.

Felix: Is that a form of punishment?

Flaco: Well, yeah. Also one of the mainheads gave him a violation. He kicked the shit out of him; he kicked him on the chest, and he [Flash] started to cry.

Felix: Well, how is sending him to a different turf a form of punishment?

Flaco: Because he has to start the turf. There is nothing happening there. The turf doesn't have a reputation for being a business corner. So, it's going to take him some time to give it a reputation.

Felix: I take it that Flash is a dealer and not a distributor.

Flaco: Right, he buys and sells for himself. He was taking advantage of his power. Everybody else is busting their ass off every day and doing it together, you know, like that. And he didn't want to cooperate, so he got a violation and a punishment. I'm sure he will learn from this.

This chapter outlines the sequential career patterns of this group of Puerto Rican youth gang members. Youngsters undergo a gradual process of learning specific skills and establishing a network of relationships with significant members of the organization in order to become dealers. The gang serves as a street academy, supplying would-be dealers with avenues and personnel from which to learn these necessary aptitudes. To be sure, drug dealing represents far more than simply a spontaneous activity carried out by youngsters who are given an amount of drugs to sell. Drug dealing is a job, and, like other jobs, it must be learned over time. It requires a considerable investment of time to acquire skills, plan, and operate systematically.

Most of the street-level dealers I studied did not achieve the status of independent dealers. The few that did remained small-time operators, making only enough to stay in business; "I'm only making enough to survive" was a recurrent theme. In some cases, independent dealers felt "off" and returned to work for distributors as hired dealers.

6

Future Aspirations and Limitations: The Catch-22 Consequence of Gang Participation

What becomes of the members of the Diamonds who fail to reach the level of distributor? What do they do with their lives? Where do they go from here? This final chapter addresses these questions. It begins with an exploration of those particular skills or capacities youngsters have gained as gang members and which they plan to use for getting ahead in the world. It then examines the various mental pictures members of the Diamonds have developed toward conventional work—about the kinds of jobs they wish to do and those they have come to recognize as outside of their realm. The chapter then looks at how the youngsters finally become aware of their perpetual entrapment within the gang's occupational structure, decide to rebel against this condition, and develop various forms of resistance in opposition to this system of exploitation.

═ *"I Can Do It"*

"I'm looking for a job to make me some money. I have flipped hamburgers, mopped floors, and done other jobs, but the good jobs—they are not there. Not for us, anyway. People are always saying that we should get a job—but who says that the only jobs we can do are in the restaurants or in selling clothes and shoes and stuff like? What do these jobs pay, anyway? Even when I go and apply for one of these jobs, the first thing people ask me is about my high school diploma. Then, if I lie and tell them that I graduated, they tell me that they can hire me to work twenty-five or thirty hours a week. These people think that we are stupid. You know, we don't need, . . . we don't want those jobs. We can do other things, you know, other jobs, but the jobs where these things are found are not available for people like us. It's as simple as that."

Rafael's evaluation of the job situation he is facing in today's service economy is similar to that expressed by other members of the Diamonds. Rafael and his friends express a feeling of deep frustration over the job prospects available to youngsters in to- day's labor market. It is interesting to discover, nonetheless, that, although these youngsters are deeply aware of the structural constraints that directly affect their capacity to secure perma- nent and rewarding employment, their outlook is relatively opti- mistic. Members of the Diamonds have not lost their initiative, their self-reliance, and their instinctive feeling that they might be able to change their individual and social circumstances by uti- lizing their "street smarts." These youngsters see their present lives and their futures in a relatively favorable light, believing that gang participation has equipped them with insights and skills with which they can improve the conditions of their lives.

Felix: What things did you learn from the gang that are useful today?

Lobo: I got taught how to make business—how to associate with people when selling. I can take that and put it to good use.

Felix: Explain to me exactly what you were taught.

Lobo: I learned that, if I'm selling something or whatever I got to get rid of, I never get rid of it for the price they're asking. And I never set a price; I let them set a price. I made my business where it would be between me and that person only, and, if I wanted these customers to keep coming back, and I promised them something, they would get it. I would not break any promises. And I would not go first come, first serve. If I promised this person that I get him this, I would get it for him whether he came first or not. I would do this when making business with stolen good, but with drugs I set my price and standards to sell with the club [gang] or alone.

Felix: What other things did you learn?

Lobo: Not being afraid—this is something I learned. To be in a gang you must overcome being afraid. Gang members get that taught every day in their hood. If you are going to survive living in a city like Chicago, you can't be afraid. You have to learn that. That's why some guys get beat up by their own gang—it's like you have to toughen them up. I think that a person going into a gang is like someone going into the army: You have to train them, and usually they both come out the same way.

Felix: What do you mean by that?

Lobo: I wouldn't say you come out of the army as a crazy, but you come out obsessed with violence, sometimes incurable. The same thing is true with the gang. You come out like if you were in a battle, too. You always want to settle your problems through violence. You might come out with a bullet still in your head or some parts of your body missing. In the army, like in the gang, you get taught to overcome that fear of being afraid. For many drugs was the answer for overcoming their fear of being afraid.

As it did for Lobo, gang participation contributed enormously to Eddie's transformation into a highly competent and crafty person. Flaco claims to have developed a particular wisdom that distinguishes him from his neighborhood peers, whom he perceives as having accepted a way of life that offers them only false hope. Flaco is highly critical of his "conformist peers" for not attempting to change, reject, or manipulate people or rules for their own ends. He thinks that when they do try they always follow prescribed means of manipulation, such as "acceptable deviance." He says, "I think that the most important thing I learned from the guys was to be smart about the streets, to take advantage of the many opportunities they offer. For example, in order to make money in the streets you need to be a good talker—to be able to develop a rap so that people can take you seriously."

"A major problem with a lot of people is that they don't know how to talk. They are not ever taught the importance of being able to use what they say to convince people of what they want. To me good talk is money. I think I'm going to be a good businessman. I got what it takes. I have several friends who are not gangbangers. They sometimes act very stupid. They're dorks, you know. They don't know how to get over. I tried helping them sometimes, but they tell me that they don't like the way I do some things. They feel my way is wrong or that what I do is against their way and against the law. They're so stupid to believe that the law is on their side. Anyway, every time I said something about the way they did things we ended up in an argument, so I don't bother with them anymore. I don't think that they are going to get anywhere doing things their way. That way doesn't pay."

For Benjy learning survival and anticipating the actions of individuals represent the major abilities he has acquired from gang participation—both of which he believes are essential ingredients for organizing his life. He says, "Well, survival of the streets is different from surviving from school and things like that. There's two types of survival: as a citizen, working, paying your taxes; and then there's survival, as with only working with the little money you have, hanging around, taking your chances, doing favors for other people. Take, for instance, the situation between gangs and drugs. These two things go hand in hand because it's a business, and that's what brings the money in and brings more corruption, but that's what people must do and invest in. When you're in a gang you take your chances selling drugs. What I learned to do is to reduce the risk factor involved in drug selling. I do take chances, because when you sell you're taking a big chance of getting busted by the cops, but I also learned to treat people good so they can serve as your watchdogs. In other businesses people don't really give a fuck about customers. You know, these large businesses like Sears, Marshall Field—they treat customers any way they want because they know that, if the customers don't like it, there will always be someone else who will. I don't conduct my business that way. I try working close with my clients. I guess that I don't have the luxury to be like that because the competition in the streets is really big; it's everywhere. So, if I don't show some kind of care for my customers, they go to someone else. And you know that I can't afford for that to happen, so I'm cool with them."

"Another thing is that you can't get sloppy about what you're doing. I really believe that you need to know what other people are thinking about. Sometimes I found this way of doing things useful. You have to think ahead a lot. And that's something that gave me an extra edge over people, because I always tried to anticipate what was going to happen before I did something. If there's one thing I've learned it's that, if someone asks you a question or someone tells you to go somewhere, let your yes be a yes and a no be a no. If you're gonna tell someone maybe, just tell them yes or no. This thing of trying to be in the middle doesn't work. The way to be able to answer yes or no is to know what that person wants from you. So, you study him; you can't say yes to him the first time you meet him. You must study him for a long period of time, and only then you can give him a definite answer."

In effect, Lobo, Flaco, Benjy, and other members of the Diamonds argue that they have gained the aggressiveness, intelligence, and cunning necessary for making it in a society where they were rendered obsolete even before they could pursue meaningful conventional roles. To them gang participation has fostered the development of a string of business experiences and interpersonal skills essential for fulfilling their aspirations. In other words, in the minds of these youngsters the gang has operated as a training school, furnishing them with the know-how to survive and move ahead in a society that offers them few opportunities for developing their individual talents.

It is also clear that success goes to those gang members who are innovative in dealing with what they have at hand. In some respects the gang culture does not differ dramatically from conventional life: Both require intelligence and entrepreneurial skills. Moreover, the two require personal energy and aggressiveness.

═ Future Hopes

Indeed, any one of us who spends enough time with these youngsters can only be impressed with their survival skills, including, in particular, their craftiness when dealing with people on the streets. After observing this group of young men and their behavior over time I became interested in learning how they were planning to use their street smarts. Do they truly believe that this knowledge can be useful for realizing their life goals? How are their skills going to be used? What are the goals these youngsters believe they are capable of reaching?

In the following exchange Carmelo provides us with a glance at the world some of these young people often talk about and aspire to.

Felix: Where are you now, insofar as the way you live and look at things around you?

Carmelo: I'm not satisfied with where I am right now—not at all. I have higher goals set for myself. I got a job; it's not bad money, but there's something in me that says that I can get much more further ahead than I am right now.

Felix: And what do you hope to accomplish?

Carmelo: Money wise?

Felix: Is that what you're referring to?

Carmelo: I can't give no definite number. Maybe I mean something else!

Felix: Are you referring to reaching a certain level of lifestyle?

Carmelo: Yeah, that's what it is. Right now I got my own apartment, saving for my own home. I guess I'm chasing the dream.

Felix: Are you saying that you have the same aspirations as everyone else in the society?

Carmelo: Look! I got a Polo shirt on. Look at the Polo shirt I got on. I got Reeboks on—I guess that's what it is. But it's weird. Somehow something tells me that I will have my house before I have my career. You know what I'm saying? I don't know. . . . That's the way I see it going.

When Coco talks about future aspirations he usually mentions the idea of "going legit." He sees himself earning and saving substantial amounts of money, which he plans to invest in the purchase of a conventional business. He says, "There are some guys who bought themselves a business after saving their drug money. I know one guy who is the owner of a car wash. Now, that's a good business because cars always get dirty, and people don't want to be seen in a dirty car. I could live like that. Or I won't mind saving me enough cash to buy a bar—you know, one of those real nice bars that attract people with money. I don't mean just any tavern like the ones we have so many of around here. There is one not too far from here that has a real good clientele."

"The real trick about these kinds of businesses that I'm talking about is that you have to be real cool; otherwise, the police will bust you. The law is out there always looking to see who is going into business because they got hip that people are using drug money and going legit. I don't think that there is nothing wrong with that. The problem is that some of these guys continue selling even after they go legit. I plan to be clean if I make it to that level. I won't need to sell drugs anymore. That could ruin my business and future."

Going legit also appears in Tony's future plans. "I don't know," he says, "What else can you do? You work all this time; you make money; you spend it; sometimes you save a little. But with the kind of money we make we have to spend it. Who is going to believe that we made all this money working at McDonalds? The thing to do is spend it. So, I decided that, if I'm going to spend what I make, I'm going to buy me something that can make me more money, and I want legal money. This is why I've been thinking about going into business. I'm not sure the kind of business, but the thing people do around here is to open up a bar, nightclubs—those are really popular—or a car wash. Those things all sound all right, but I think the law is getting hip about them. And they are beginning to make their busts. I know I want to get something—I just don't know exactly what now. I guess, when I get all the money that I need I'll think about it more seriously."

Lobo also hopes to get ahead and believes that education might be his vehicle for success. He has been relying on the special commitment his girlfriend has devoted to assisting him through this extremely challenging and difficult process. He says, "Well now, after going through all I've gone through—the pain, and putting my mom and everybody through all hell. . . . I've made them suffer a lot, spending the time that I did in the joint, and then watching everybody else leading a happy life and going to school and doing things, like getting a class ring. I've always wanted one, but I can't get one until I graduate. So, I just recently got one. See, I wanted all these small, little things, like a prom and to graduate on stage and a yearbook, and I want to be known in my high school, but what high school? What high school will take me? I'm over twenty years old—what school is gonna take me? So, I thought I'd get myself together. I've come to realize the shit I've been into. I've realized the mistakes I made."

"I've been seeing a girl for some time now, and she's one that's been putting up with my shit for a long time. So, all the way until now I've been seeing her—it's going to be almost four years now—and the relationship has just been too good. So, she's got these plans, like right after high school we go to college together and maybe get married after college and stuff, so, I'm willing to go for it. This is the first girl that I've ever seen that has put up with me, besides my family."

"Yeah, and a career would top my life. So, I want to go and finish from here. Once I get back to school, that is going to make me want to go for the next thing, which is college. I dropped out of high school since I couldn't stick to something straight and follow rules. Now I realize that, and college will be different. I will be straight and go for something that not too many people where I'm from go for: a four-year bachelor's degree. So, I'm gonna go for the whole four years and take up what I know best, which is drawing. Whether it's freehand, graphic, commercial arts, or drafting, or whatever—that I'll decide later, but it'll be in that field. I'm also interested in business, and my family has always been wanting to open a business and doing this and that, so I wouldn't mind getting something together and opening a business—maybe a sign business or something like making neon signs or whatever. So, that's just what I'm aiming for."

Although members of the Diamonds are optimistic about realizing their dreams, many are very fearful that they will end up like the adults around them. They want to avoid experiencing the severe economic deprivation and exploitation they have witnessed family members, friends, and neighbors having to endure over time. Youngsters have come to assume that repeating this experience of work inequality will only indicate their incapacity for putting into efficient use the various skills and shrewdness they claim to have learned as members of the Diamonds.

Rafael talks about growing up seeing his father work from "sunrise to sundown" and not being able to improve the conditions of the family. His description is a portrayal of the "long-term poor": the kind of worker who has been employed for most of his or her productive life but who has never moved beyond the level of bare subsistence. When speaking about his future Rafael seems petrified at the prospect of repeating this experience: "I come from a family that believed in hard work and getting ahead the old-fashioned way. My mom didn't work much because she was at home taking care of my little brothers and sisters. Besides, my father was too old-fashioned and didn't think that his wife should be working. So, he did the working. But, you know, I admired him a lot and still do. Hey, like you have to, because he worked all kinds of hours and worked hard because he always looked tired. He was so beat-up from work that all he did when he got home was eat and sleep. Sometimes I wonder how he made all those kids. For real, man, like, where did he get the energy? But, anyway, like, look at our family after so many years. Hey, I'm not complaining, but what did he get from all that work?

We're still in the same situation, except that now he can't work as many hours as before because he's older and the factory cut back a lot. . . . I don't want that. I got to find me a way to do better than that."

"I don't mean to sound like if I'm lazy or something. I do want to work, and I plan to work, but the work I want to do has to have some security. If I'm going to work for all the years people spend working, then I expect to receive what I'm entitled to. My father was never paid for the kind of work he put into his factory job. And I don't think what I'm asking is too much or unfair. Like everybody else, I think that I deserve certain things that I work for. But right now those jobs won't do."

Carmelo, on the other hand, expresses anger over the closing of the factory where his father worked and the fact that his father lost much of the pension into which he had invested a great deal of money. "It's really unfair," he says, "but I guess the world is unfair. These people abused and took advantage of my father and I'm sure this happened to many others. I will not work for no one—that's not going to happen to me. You know, its like these businesses in the neighborhood—they can close down whenever they want to. They put up these signs saying that they are going out of business and stuff like that. Well, a few weeks later you see the same merchandise in the store; you see the same people working in the store. What kind of shit is that? So, factories do the same. Whenever they get into problems with money they announce that they are going bankrupt, close down, and they don't have to be responsible for the workers. Hey, that's not for me. There should be a law against those practices. I talk to the fellas about this all the time, and this is one reason why we have no faith at all in the ways things are done here. Like, who *can* be after seeing so much?"

While recalling the enormous amount of daily work his mother carried out both at a factory and at home, Red speaks of his desire to remove this painful experience from his memory: "You know, my dad worked, and I'm sure he worked hard—but not as hard as my mother. She would get up in the morning, fix us breakfast, and send us off to school, and she would go to work. She would come home and do the same thing over again. Most of the times my father wasn't home, so she had to do everything. There were times she would bring home some work from the factory. She would stay up working on that stuff even after we went to sleep. Talking about having it hard—hey, I'm looking for something very different."

In addition, other members of the Diamonds are alarmed about the prospects of having a lower standard of living than their parents and other adults they have known. Youngsters are keenly aware that this first generation of immigrants were severely handicapped by lacking fluency in the English language and understanding about the larger urban culture in the United States. Nonetheless, even as newcomers, the parents and adult friends of some of the Diamonds managed to do fairly well for themselves.

Carmelo mentions a neighbor who worked in the airport as a truck driver delivering food to the airplanes. He describes this man as a very proud person: "He knew where he was going to earn a living every day. And he was proud of it, too." I asked Carmelo for his opinion of this type of work, and his response provides a glimpse of the youngsters' apprehension about falling short of the achievements realized by their parents and others from this early immigrant generation: "I think that [his neighbor's work] was OK. Besides, he was promoted to a higher job there. The fact that he did not know how to speak English and the fact that he was a high school dropout—hey, that's not bad. I couldn't even find that kind of job myself. He got this job through a friend from his hometown in Puerto Rico. He would tell us that story a lot. He wanted us to know how hard he struggled to get to where he was. But I don't have those kinds of friends. My friends, you know, don't have those kinds of jobs or those connects."

In a different way Rafael expresses similar misgivings about the idea of failing to equal a relative's success: "I have an uncle that came to live with us from Puerto Rico. He stayed with us for about two or three years. I became his favorite nephew. So, we always talked and spent a lot of time together. We would go to the park and things like that. Anyway, he worked for a very long time at this company. He had different jobs, until one day he was promoted to cook. He did not start working in the kitchen, but that's where he ended up. I think some people think that these kinds of jobs are no big deal. My uncle really likes his work, and he makes a lot of money. To tell you the truth, I won't mind doing that kind of work. But I don't think that I'll ever be able to find a job that pays the kind of money my uncle is making. It's really tough, man. Can you believe that my uncle and other people like him are doing so good? He always told me to do better than him. He was always encouraging me to stay in school. He would talk to me about getting good grades and stuff like that. But he did not know about the kind of shit we had to put up with in school—with our teachers, with the bangers, you know. Look at me now. What can I tell you? How can you explain it? There's hope. Me and my friends are not going to throw our arms up in the air and give up. Something is going to happen, I hope."

═ Disillusionment

Overall, the theme of "making it" is a very important one for the young people who are members of the Diamonds. As the various accounts above indicate, these members believe they have developed aptitudes and strategies for realizing their life ambitions, some of which can be said to be desired by most teenagers in the United States. In effect, for members of the Diamonds the so-called American dream may be deferred, but it certainly is not dead. Achieving the dream may appear to be much tougher for them today than for many other youngsters or when compared to earlier generations of teenagers, yet members of the Diamonds are far from giving up on it.

It is also true that making it or getting ahead, for people from low socioeconomic and minority racial and ethnic backgrounds and for women never has happened cheaply. All of these groups, at one time or another, have been easy targets of victimization and exploitation. Many of us know firsthand or have heard through the news media of cases involving poor families and individuals who were sold poor-quality merchandise at extremely high prices. We have seen or read, for example, about older people being charged exorbitant amounts of money for minor house repairs. Several cases were reported earlier in this chapter of factory closing and of workers not receiving benefits to which they were entitled. Many women have been forced into sexual acts as preconditions for keeping their jobs or for promotion. There are many similar experiences in which economically powerful "outsiders" have taken advantage of poor and young people and women.

Unfortunately, the painful reality is that sometimes these cases of humiliation and suffering are engendered by the very same mechanisms created to remove conditions of injustice. That is to say, there are times when strategies and activities developed by individuals and groups serve to reproduce rather than overcome circumstances of inequality. For Flaco, Tito, Lobo, Frankie, Coco, and the others the Diamonds represent one "indigenous cultural development" that had a backfiring effect on their lives. For these youngsters the gang did not serve as the leverage necessary for improving their life chances in society, as they had earlier envisioned. Instead of functioning as a progressive and liberating agent capable of transforming and correcting the youngsters' economic plight, the gang assisted in reinforcing it.

Understandably, members of the Diamonds working at street-level dealing are profoundly disappointed with the way things have turned out for them. During our conversations some of them demonstrated an unwillingness to acknowledge the actual outcome produced by their participation in the Diamond's drug-dealing business. I understood clearly that their inclination was to reflect only on the positive dimensions of gang membership and participation, for they do not want to recognize the problems and negative results stemming from the gang's business operations.

Several youngsters took great pains to establish the neutral role played by the gang in determining the future economic outcome of its members. The explanation most readily given was that there are moments when the gang is prevented from achieving its productive capabilities by forces outside its control. The argument essentially revolves around a perception that the gang's course of action is heavily influenced by what's taking place outside its immediate surroundings. It is not that the gang intentionally wants to subjugate its members; rather, it is more the case that external conditions and forces press heavily upon the organization's capacity to provide opportunities for advancement.

This attitude was captured in a telephone conversation I had with Flaco, in which he explained how constant police disruptions of strategic weekly meetings prevent the gang from carrying out its normal business operations. These disruptions, in turn, are believed to be a reason why members cannot enjoy the "fruit of their labor." The day was Saturday, 21 April 1990. I had called Flaco to remind him of the meeting we had arranged for that afternoon. I did not want to experience another letdown like the last one, when he did not show up. I called and found Flaco still in bed. He answered grudgingly. I apologized for having woken him and reminded him about our meeting. Before I could finish he was responding, though his answer had absolutely nothing to do with what I had just said. With a nervous voice he said, "Oh, man, Felix, you should have been there last night. The law came from every side. They busted in the crib of Spade where we were meeting, but since we were alerted by Joey, who was on guard, we all escaped. I ran down the alley, and so did everyone else. It seemed that there were thousands of cops. There were cars everywhere. I think they got Red because he wasn't back later on when we got together again."

"You see, this is the stuff I've been telling you about. The police makes their own rules—now they can break into your place whenever they want. What this means is that they will catch more of us, and we are going to start using more cash to get people out of jail. And those that get out are going to have to do work for a long time to pay for what the mainhead spends on them. How are we supposed to advance? We want to, but we can't because the law is on our tail now more than any other time before."

Flaco was trying to provide an explanation that shields the gang from having to assume responsibility for the present economic plight of its members. What Flaco appeared to be saying was that it was not that the gang does not want to see its members get ahead but, rather, that the gang must be responsible for its own maintenance and the well-being of its members—responsibilities that require unanticipated monetary expenditures. And, of course, the more money spent for the protection of gang members, the less there is for members to use in ways that could improve their economic conditions.

Other members do not see things happening the way Flaco described. During certain moments when they feel most distressed their reflections about why things have gone sour point to a more permanent problem that sounds like an indictment of the gang—specifically, its refusal to help them improve their life chances. They believe the gang is the culprit—that, by design, it established an operation to benefit only the chiefs and mainheads. These members describe having undergone a long and agonizing process of developing a consciousness as a family—as a community sharing common visions and goals—only to be betrayed or, at best, to be treated as marginal workers. They have become desperate, angry, and sometimes even hostile toward the very same people who had promised to "take care" of them.

In the following account Elf clearly expresses his disappointment at the negative aftermath of gang membership: "I'm really in a bind. There is nothing for me. I don't know what to do. I'm confused. I've been with the gang for a long time, and look at me now. There was no one as down on the gang as I was. I've done some dirty shit when other people have come after us. Like,

I've sacrificed my life. I've done more than what people asked me. I've spent time in jail. Everything bad has happened to me. What do I have to show for it? I don't have no money. I got a beat-up car. I don't have my own crib. Where do I go from here? I want to do things, but I don't know how. We spend so much time in the streets, in the gang, trying to do things for people—and what happens?"

Carmelo voices anger over the crushing sense of defeat he feels about being part of a gang that promised hope instead.

Felix: What do you think of your present situation in terms of liking or approving of it?

Carmelo: I'm not sure I can say I like it. I have built a good relationship with the guys, and for me that's really important. I've been with them for a long time, and, as I told you before, they are my family. We do everything together, and we care for one another.

Felix: What about your situation, as you see it, in economic terms?

Carmelo: Well, when I first joined that was one thing I had in mind. I wanted to make some money to make something of myself. I used to see guys with the big cars and the ladies, and I thought everyone was like that. But those guys are the mainheads. You know, they are the suppliers, and there are only a few of them around. But when I would see these guys I always thought that I wanted to be like them or at least make my share to get the things I always wanted, like they did.

Felix: And what happened?

Carmelo: Not much. I didn't get there. I guess I've still waiting for things to happen for me.

Felix: How hopeful are you that things will work out for you?

Carmelo: Well, I just don't know. I want to believe that it's going to come my way, but I don't know. I mean, how long must I wait? What about my friends? I have friends in prison who never got what they were looking for. I did not expect things to work this way. I get very pissed off sometimes, but the gang is like everything else. It's like working for McDonalds and these other places around here where you find all of these Latino teenagers and young people working at.

Felix: And how is that?

Carmelo: You can only get so far. Once you reach a certain level there's nowhere else to go. That's it. In the gang we got as high as possible. We advanced as far as we were supposed to. The thing is that we never expected it to be this way. They told us about the gangbanging, about the Vs, but the economic side—well, they just said that we could make a lot of money. It was left at that. We never bothered to question it. We didn't have to; after all, here were these guys who looked like if they had won the lottery. Now we know.

In a similar way, Tito indicates having spent too much time in the gang without receiving any tangible benefits. Like others, he feels trapped and unable to do the things he wants. "Well, I have a lot of things that I have to look towards," he says, "and gangbanging isn't getting me anywhere. Like, I need a diploma, but I got kicked out of school because I was hanging out in the neighborhood selling drugs. And the one thing that sucks about gangbanging is that you get locked up a lot. You get taken to jail a lot just for anything—just for hanging out on the corner. You sell drugs, and you get caught for that. And I was going to jail a lot of times for all kinds of things I was doing for the gang. I finally realized, you know, I shouldn't be doing these things. Why am I going to jail so much? What am I getting from the gang in return?"

"I became very pissed off. But I think I was more pissed off with myself than with the gang because I let many of these things happen. I could have avoided them. So, I started thinking about things that I could do that were going to be done for me, and I was going to do these things myself. Like, I want to go to the marines pretty soon, and I have to get my high school diploma and get past school, because when I was in high school the reason I failed was because I was hanging out with the guys."

Why did things turn out so differently than members of the Diamonds had anticipated? Why was the gang not capable of delivering the goods its members had desired? The decision by Flaco, Lobo, Benjy, Tito, and the others to join the Diamonds was inspired in part by the possibility of establishing a business. They had come to believe that the gang possessed the necessary components through which they could realize this goal and other associated individual aspirations. But these young people had not anticipated being relegated to the status of a dependent class of workers. (Since they had been very young and only knew bits and pieces of gang life, perhaps it is more appropriate to say that they could not have anticipated this outcome.) While youngsters thought that true communalism and equality could be achieved, the fact is that within the gang a class hierarchy exists and it is they who fill its bottom ranks. This being the case, a reconceptualization of the actual functions of the gang clearly indicates that it involves not only the training of these youngsters into competent street-level dealers but also the preparation of workers as individuals who develop and hold basic principles and attitudes that contribute to maintaining the power structure within the organization.

How is this system of power differentiation produced and maintained? What are the specific ingredients used by the gang's dominant class to ensure that street-level dealers remain subordinate?

═ Cultural Ideology

In chapter 3 I examined the process through which members of the Diamonds are systematically socialized by older and influential gang members (usually the mainheads or representatives of the mainheads). I described how they develop the types of personal demeanor, modes of self-preservation, self-image, and social identification which are essential cultural ingredients for becoming gang members. An additional, yet covert, feature of the socialization process has to do with upholding the authority and power of the mainheads and, in doing so, positioning the street-level dealers in subordinate occupational positions. In other words, the gang's dominant class is solely responsible for the production and reinforcement of a culture and dictates what it means to be a member of the Diamonds; of course, its definition is consistent with its interests. Moreover, the mainheads' interpretation of the social world seeks to present their economic and political interests not as arbitrary but as necessary and natural elements of the gang organization.

Thus, one major instrument for maintaining street-level dealers at the bottom of the gang's occupational hierarchy is their acceptance of the gang's cultural ideology. That street-level dealers are socialized to hold the mainheads in the highest esteem is evidenced by the views and impressions the former expresses of the latter.

When speaking about their distributors members of the Diamonds often view them as individuals who have paid their dues by remaining with the gang for a very long period time and, thus, have gained the respect of other members and vast knowledge about the city's drug distribution network. The distributors are perceived as being very intelligent and cunning for having accumulated the capital necessary to purchase bulk quantities of drugs and going into business. Lobo says of his distributor, "I can understand why this guy is the way he is. Hey, he is the one that got busted all those times. He probably spent all kinds of time in prison. And now he is going to cash in on that. That's just how it is. Sometimes he would tell us stories—you know, stories about how he spent his life with the gang and holding the gang together or the times he took the rap for some other guy. We all got impressed with his record, and we started looking up to him for that."

On another occasion Lobo adds the following impressions of the distributor: "Every gang has a least one distributor. There are times when a section may not have one, . . . well, these guys then buy from another distributor from the larger gang or from another section. My guess is that the older guys take trips to Florida or meet people halfway. I heard some guys going downtown for the stash. Some of these people are supposed to be in real estate big-time, restaurants, and stuff. But it's through some big business, and the owner of the business was handling the stuff. But this is all done by the older guys. The younger ones never got into this; they couldn't. It's the older ones who know what the business is all about, who are making money and living a nice life. They also know those who live the fast life. They are into communicating with one another and making money. We all respect that."

In the following discussion I had with Flaco he expresses similar views of the distributor. We were talking about circumstances involving a youngster who could not afford to pay an amount of money for drugs he had been fronted.

Felix: What happens to this guy who cannot come up with the money to pay the mainhead?
Flaco: He's got to. If he doesn't, he gets an ugly V.
Felix: Is that fair?
Flaco: Of course, it is. He can't do that shit to the mainhead. We need him [the mainhead] because he's the one that gives us the stuff to sell. So, if he doesn't have the money, he can't buy nothing.
Felix: What about other people—can you go to them for stuff?
Flaco: No, we can't. We work with the people in our gang. We

learn to give them respect. They're the ones that helped us in the first place. So, we work for them. We do what they tell us.

Felix: And when do they tell you what to do?

Flaco: Well, that's what we learn as Pee Wees. They don't come up to us and tell us this or that. We already know that. Besides, they need to keep away, clear from the law. They hardly come to the corner. That's one way of protecting them. They don't come around as much.

Felix: So, when do you make contact with your distributor?

Flaco: Most of the time when he brings us the stuff himself or when he collects the money. That's about it.

Indeed, the cultural ideology forced upon members of the Diamonds encourages a system that distorts reality in order to serve the interests of the organization's dominant class. By appearing to be impartial and neutral transmitters of the benefits of gang culture, the mainheads are able to promote inequality in the name of fairness. It is through the exercise of real and symbolic power that the Diamonds's leadership imposes its ruling control over street-level dealers.

Minimum Wage

To be sure, distributors hold a virtual monopoly over the purchase and supply of drugs sold by members of the Diamonds. Distributors exercise great influence over street-level dealers through their control over drug sources. A single distributor may have as many as ten youngsters working for him on a regular or periodic basis. The salary paid to each youngster depends on the type of relationship that is established. Any time that the distributor believes that an individual dealer is not making enough money, he will sever the relationship by refusing to supply him. Along with their monopoly over the supplies of cocaine and marijuana, the ability to hire and fire employees and establish the terms of salaries endows distributors with a considerable amount of influence over and control of youngsters working at street-level dealing.

In effect, the low wages earned by street-level dealers serves as another major explanation for their entrapment at the bottom of the gang's business structure. Contrary to official and popular belief, street-level employment—that is, the work performed by youngsters who are hired by the gang distributor or supplier—yields only modest wages. Through gang-related drug-dealing work youngsters' earnings amount to mere survival income. They work from day to day or week to week generating the kind of salary that allows them to purchase only some of life's basic necessities. They do not mismanage their money, nor do they spend it on lavish and extravagant frills. The fact is that this group of workers are laboring for meager wages.

As long as the power for determining workers' salaries lies in the hands of the distributor, it is expected that the amount paid to street-level dealers will always remain at a level that will ensure their continuing dependence. When wages paid are meager the likelihood that street-level dealers will advance economically and possibly go out on their own are substantially reduced. This, in turn, will ensure the distributor with an available and controlled pool of workers with experience and good selling skills.

Benjy worked for his distributor for two years, never advancing beyond the occupation of hired dealer. The salary Benjy earned enabled him to stay above water. "I made enough to make it," he explains. "It wasn't enough to go out and buy fancy gym shoes, like a lot of guys. There's some street corners that just have better business than others, and most of the guys go out and buy gold chains and gym shoes, and that's all it is. It's like, who's got the hottest gym shoes on the block? It's like the trend that teenagers and gangs have."

"I was making, say—out of one hundred dollars I made twenty-five dollars. I usually took twenty dollars for two days, and I made sure I spent, like, five dollars on a nickel bag for relaxation and the other five dollars was to buy a big meal, and I ate it, and the rest of the time I'd get high on my friend's supply or on my own. I'd take a few dollars extra and get high or go around spraypainting or doing things that we had nothing better to do after we made the money. We couldn't go back and keep buying and buying 'cause there were times the person didn't always have any. There was always a time to gangbang, and there was a time to make money—that's how it is."

Lobo's wages are far better than Benjy's, though he feels his earnings are not sufficient for any upward mobility.

Felix: You indicated working for a distributor—what kind of money are you making?

Lobo: It all depends on the hours you work. During school I worked—and after school from four to ten or a summer night. And also it depends on what you were selling. Some guys sell acid, some have the cane; some have the bow. I started selling drugs where I would be bringing sometimes, after working from four to ten, about two-hundred and fifty to three-hundred dollars from what he gave me to sell.

Felix: What was your take from that amount?

Lobo: That would be all the money out of all the little bags he would give me to sell. I'd go up and take him the money. There's times when it would be lower. I would be taking him some money and a couple of bags that were left over that I couldn't sell. My cut out of this would be from three to four dollars on every bag I sold, so I would walk out with seventy or eighty duckies [bucks]—sometimes less, sometimes more, depending on what I sold. As far as selling cocaine, that's always a little bit more. Quarters would run about twenty-five dollars a few years ago. Now sometimes fifteen or twenty dollars. At times, when it gets real, really dry we go up to thirty or thirty-five dollars a quarter. People get so desperate that they would buy it, only because it was getting real dry.

Felix: So, what you're saying is that you were not making that much money?

Lobo: That's just the thing. You make money for yourself and your pocket, and it's not that much. At times it could be. If you could really move to sell and put in a lot of hours, you could make money. But in my case I never left the corner. I was really . . . "You wanna buy it? No?" then I wouldn't talk the person into it. You got your gangbangers who would persuade you into it. They'd do whatever they could to get the money. And they work from sunset to sundown. I really wasn't into that.

And in the following account Tito provides information about the kind of salary he was earning as a street-level dealer: "For, like . . . I stole cars and stuff like that for a good nine to ten months. It went pretty easy until I got caught. But when I did time I didn't want to do it no more because the cops will always be on me. They would always be watching me. So, I sold drugs, like about a good two years. I sold drugs, and I never sold it so much that I got greedy, and I had a lot of money. I did it, like, when I was starting to get low on cash or just to go and make more money, and then spend my profit and take the money I put into it, and that's how I got more money. It was so much easier, and it went so much better, too, because I didn't have to do it all the time. I just did it once in a while when I needed money. And it was better—it was more easier—since you don't have to drive around with it or nothing. You could always stash it somewhere, and, if the cops stop you and search you, they don't find nothing because it's stashed somewhere. It's easier to get it by the law than stealing cars or other things."

"I stopped selling because I got a job that was paying me pretty good money, and I didn't have the time anymore to be out on the corner selling. So, they were paying me like two-hundred-fifty dollars a week, and it was all right, and I would work full-time. It was, like, from seven in the morning until three in the afternoon. And there went most of my day. When I went home I was tired. I just wanted to eat and go to sleep for a little while. When I came outside it was already night, and there's not too many people out at night looking for drugs; it's usually in the early hours of the evening and the mornings and afternoons. So, since I'm still with the fellows, I just hang out. We do the things we always did, except that I don't have to sell drugs anymore."

═ Money Liabilities

Not being able to experience economic advancement through gang participation also resulted from the monetary indebtedness street-level dealers would accrue for favors performed by distributors. In particular, the common practice of the bailout, wherein bond money for securing the release of jailed gang members is fronted by distributors, represents a leading procedure for forcing and maintaining youngsters indebtedness over long periods of time. This is so because one condition of the bail calls for immediate repayment; once youngsters are let out of jail they are expected to pay the distributor the amount invested for their release. What this means for the released gang member is working overtime until he has accumulated the amount necessary to "clear his credit account" with the distributor. A youngster could work for a month or two only to see all the earnings go directly to paying his debt. Subsistence during this period is facilitated by the goodwill of other members—in particular, by those individuals who have formed very strong relationships as "brothers." Other forms of sustenance are given by way of loans. Settling various financial liabilities, then, comes to represent the purpose of the work carried out by street-level dealers at certain periods of time.

Because the probability of being apprehended by the police and subsequent jailing is very high for youngsters involved in street-dealing work, several members of the Diamonds I met had gone through periods of perpetual liability. Flaco is one such youngster. The following notes from Friday, 6 April 1990, illustrates his predicament. Today was somewhat unusual compared to other Fridays. It's now around 5:30 in the early evening, and the hood appears very quiet. I was hoping to meet some of the guys, for the weather is getting nicer, and the action always tend to pick up beginning in this part of the year. One can see the customers more often than when it is cold. During the cold months most of the likely customers appear in cars, but when the weather begins to warm up the streets become filled with many buyers on foot. But nothing is happening today. I drove around several times, and no one was around. I left and came back several hours later, and it was still the same scene of an empty street. I left and returned the next day. I saw Red, who told me that the police had conducted a raid early in the day on Friday to remove the dealers from the streets. I asked for Flaco, Benjy, and the others, and he said that he thought they all had gotten busted.

I finally made contact with Flaco on Monday. He informed me that he had been arrested, along with five other friends, for disturbing the peace. "We had parked right off the curve," he said, "and we were talking when the law came. They searched us and looked into the car and then took us away because we are not supposed to have a car parked on the middle of the street. Supposedly, we were preventing other cars from going through." I asked him how he had managed to post bond so quickly. He responded by saying, "The person you work for bails you out. Anytime the person you have working for you—they always get you out. They always ask you what's your real name and everything because, I think, they expect you to get locked up, and you get their beeper number or their telephone number, and you call them because you get a phone call at the police station. And they won't get you out that day because usually they hold you until Monday, till your court hearing. Like me, they locked me on a Friday, and I called them. Then he went down there, and they would't let me out till Monday. And now, for my court hearing, he goes to the courtroom, and he gets me a lawyer and everything. They are supposed to help out."

I then asked Flaco about the money that was used for getting him out—how much it was and whether he was obligated to pay it back. To this question he answered, "Well, it doesn't matter how much it costs. Unless it's a major crime and the mainhead can't come up with the money. But here we're talking about a thousand bucks or so. But once you're out you got to pay him back. It's like a credit they give you. And they want their money quickly. So, I now must work for this guy for free. Well, it isn't for free because he got me out, but he is going to make money from me because he knew I was a good worker and reliable and always sold the stuff he gave me. That's another reason he got me out—because he knew I was good for what I was doing."

"Anyway, there was another time when this happened to me, and for a long time, maybe a month—I think it was longer than that—I was working and not making anything for me. It was difficult because sometimes I didn't have anything to eat. I could eat at home, and I did, but when you're out on the streets you try to do everything yourself. You want to show people that you can support yourself. There were times when some of my closest friends would give me a few bucks to help me out. By the time I paid the mainhead I had to start all over again. I owed all kinds of money to everybody. It's difficult shaking yourself out of this situation."

Lobo experienced similar situations. In the following account, however, he describes a fundamental financial ingredient of the bailout procedure which I heard explained in this particular way just this once. According to Lobo, bailing youngsters out of jail represents nothing more than an additional business scheme on the part of the distributors for generating additional profits themselves: "Most of them do it intending to get that guy out, but he would have to pay him back double. This is a way for him to make more money. It's like an investment: The guy would have to pay him two times what it costs to get him out of jail in the first place. I saw this happen several times. I even saw it where the big head borrowed the money from the club's [gang's] funds and was charged double for paying it back. I heard that he needed the money to pay his rent, but, instead, he went and bailed out one of the brothers. We like to help out in every way, but sometimes there isn't enough for everyone's problems. Besides, for some of the fellas this is another way of doing business."

➡ *Development of a Deviant Social Identity*

Street-level dealers' subordination also results from a fundamental element inherent in gang participation: the attachment of a "deviant social identity" by the larger society to gang members. Youngsters are socialized by the gang not to view gang participation as a deviant act. Yet the gang affords its members only partial protection from the negative judgments of the dominant culture. The actions of members of the Diamonds are perceived by the larger society (as well as by some members of local community institutions and social service agencies) as constituting a violation of conventional norms, and, as such, gang members are treated with great suspicion and disdain. In other words, to be known as a gang member means to be always perceived and treated as a deviant. Furthermore, in most cases these youngsters are treated as criminals and are, thus, deprived of basic human services and resources.

Benjy was denied enrollment in a school program because of his reputation. "I tried getting into the [school]," he explains, "but [the principal] told me that I had messed up before and he couldn't take a chance with me. I was in another program, like the one there, and I quit after a few months because I thought that I wasn't getting anything out of it. So, I guess that did it for me."

"I tried getting into my old high school because I only needed four credits to graduate, and I always wanted to graduate like everybody else, you know, walking down the aisle and with a prom to make my mother proud of me, but the principal told me that I was nineteen years old, much older than his seniors, and that he was afraid I would hurt them. He said that I had too much more experience than his seniors and that I would intimidate them, and they'd be afraid of me. He just gave me a bunch of crap, so I walked out of his office."

"Plus, my street reputation. . . . I used to be wild. I didn't take shit from nobody. That became known, and people in the neighborhood know about me. When I try telling them that I'm a changed person they don't believe me."

The same fate awaits youngsters who, out of desperation, decide to try securing employment in conventional jobs. Their gang identity serves to block potential job opportunities. A friend gave Tony a lead about a job at a local hot dog stand for which he applied and was denied employment. Tony believes that he was not hired because his social profile would have scared customers away. He says, "My friend told me about this job in the neighborhood. It was perfect. It was a couple of blocks from my house. Also, I used to work for Wendy's, so I thought I had a real good chance to get the job. I stopped by, and the guy almost flipped. I don't think that he ever expected to see one of us guys applying for a regular job, let alone a job in his place. We used to eat at his place, and we would always make fun of the straight guys working there. I never considered working at a place like that."

"One thing about the dude was that he was straight. He told me straight up that he couldn't hire me. He said that I would bring all sorts of problems to his business because too many people in the hood already knew me. I'm supposed to have a bad reputation. He also said that, if he hired me, that all of my gang friends would always be at his joint. And because of that he was going to lose all of his customers. He also told me that, if the opposition found out I working there, they might decide to shoot at me from the streets and that for sure that would be the end of his business."

Overall, several forces and conditions are responsible for maintaining street-level dealers in a state of subordination. Some of these conditions are found within the operations of the gang, and others are external to it. Both function in a way that keeps these youngsters from experiencing economic improvement.

⏤ Responses to Gang Oppression

What is interesting about members of the Diamonds involved in street-level drug dealing is that they do not passively accept their subordinate status. They have finally decided to resist these circumstances of inequality and exploitation. In the same way that during an earlier period of their life they resisted the exploitation of conventional society by looking to the gang as an instrument for improving their conditions, they now have to design a series of strategies with which to respond to their ongoing participation in the lower ranks of the gang, where job-related consequences carry the heaviest penalties, such as police apprehension and jailing and in many cases death. Once members come to recognize their entrapment—how their circumstances of inequality are, in fact, reproduced through gang participation—they begin taking action to bring about some relief.

One response adopted by some members entails limiting the time invested in gang activities, particularly hanging out. Youngsters are aware that they are required to hang out primarily to prevent rival gangs from taking over their turf. Additionally, they know that the time spent hanging out on the street block or corner determines the earning power of the mainheads or distributors. Mirroring the method of work stoppages employed by conventional workers at odds with their employers, a refusal to devote the amount of time required of them contributes to frustrating the entire process of capital accumulation for the gang's powerful elements.

Of course, this type of behavior carries severe penalties. Youngsters face disciplinary action for refusing to spend the expected time out on the streets. A violation is one form of penalty, or punishment might entail being sent out on a mission to spray-paint the walls of the opposition's turf. Another more severe assignment might be having to shoot a member of an opposition gang.

In spite of the possible hazards, some members of the Diamonds's street-level dealing scene have decided to cut back on the time spent hanging out. There is the case of Lucky, a young man I met and talked to on only one occasion. At the time of our contact I did not realize that he had been chronically absent from most of the Diamonds's activities for several months and that he was wanted by the organization. I met Lucky through another Diamond, who knew him very well and agreed not to turn him in. In our conversation Lucky informed me that he was "getting tired of doing the same thing without getting much out of it." He explained: "I want to get my life together. I want to get my life in order, but I can't because the gang was taking so much of my time. I have a kid who is eighteen months, and I want him to know that I'm his father. So, I don't come around as much because I want to spend time with him."

"I've been threatened several times. In fact, one time they were going to give me a violation, and I told them to go ahead, to get it over with because I was not scared. So, the chief said to forget it this time. I told them that I wanted to receive the kind of money I was entitled to receive, that I was working too many hours for a few bucks—that I could be making that kind of money turning hamburgers, and I would not have to worry about the cops busting me or the opposition coming after my ass. The chief said that everyone there makes the same, that I was complaining to cover the fact that I was just lazy and didn't want to get out to work and hang out."

Another young man that decided to lessen his gang participation is referred to by other members as Hipo, a street slang Spanish pronunciation of *hip*. According to stories, Hipo is hip; he is crafty and calculating. When I first met Hipo he was working part-time at a Kentucky Fried Chicken fast-food restaurant and hoping for a promotion to manager. His decision to secure a conventional job was ignited by his frustration over having to see other, more senior gang members benefit from his labor. "I'm just plain tired of being played for an idiot," he explains. "These people think that you don't know anything and that they can do with you whatever they want. What I do now is that I come around to make me a few bucks. I hang out with the guys, but that's for fun, not for work. At first the chief was messing with me about not coming around. I gave him all kinds of excuses, and he didn't believe them. Well, they were all bullshit lies; I just wanted to back away. So, I took this job frying chickens. It's no big deal, but the guys know that I'm working for real, so they tell the chief, and he says it's OK if I'm not here all the time. I really hate the job. I want to move up, but in the meantime, even though I hate that fucking job. . . . You know what it is to be turning those suckers in hot grease for four to five hours a day? I come out smelling and looking like one of them. But, anyway, as much as I hate this bullshit job, I do it because that's my ticket to be away rather than doing the dirty work for those other guys. That's slave work. We call it slaving beause that's what we do. We can't do anything but hang out for these guys, who then turn around and pay us slave wages."

For some youngsters the answer to their problem is simply to resign from the gang. They are willing to submit to the physical punishment associated with getting their V-out. Several youngsters took their V-out during the time I was carrying out my study. One such young man was Jessie. Even though he had formally left the gang, he could still be found once in a while frequenting the neighborhood and visiting his friends. Flaco introduced me to Jessie one day, and I managed to get him to talk about his decision to leave the gang. He was taken by the fact that I had been "out there with the guys where the action really is." I asked him about what he was doing, and he said that he had signed up for GED [general equivalency diploma] classes and was waiting to be called for the program. "I'm going to give straight life a chance," he said. "I'm going to get my high school diploma through the GED program. I hope it gives me a chance." I asked him if that was the reason he had quit the Diamonds, and he said, "No, not really. I didn't know what I really wanted to do. I just wanted to start by getting out. That was important because, if I didn't, I would never follow up on what I say that I would do. I would always come back only to feel angry with the whole situation."

Jessie continued; "Now, I'm on my own. Any mistakes or

problems, I can't bring them to the chief to solve. I have to deal with them myself." "What kinds of problems are you referring to?" I asked Jessie, and he answered, "Well, a lot of people are scared to get out because they are violated. I wasn't afraid. I took it like a man. And, although I got all bruised up, I'm still in one piece. But, I tell you, the problem is that people don't let you out—like the police. Every time they see you they continue to mess with you. They ask me about the boys and the Diamonds, and they call me Diamond Jessie. They don't leave me alone. They laugh at me and say that, once a gangbanger, always a gangbanger. So, they are going to treat me like if I was still a gangbanger."

"Then there is the opposition. Since I'm known, you know, I got a record for doing some bad shit to the opposition. I can't go into some neighborhoods because they too always will treat me like a Diamond. So, in a way the police are right because in their eyes you are always a gangbanger. Anyway, I don't want to get ambushed by the opposition, so I stay far from them. I'm not going to be an easy target for them."

"So, this is my situation now. In a way I'm out of the gang because the Diamonds know and recognize that officially I'm not one of them, but, outside, people still see me like always. But this is a consequence for what I did. I messed up some people, and people don't forget that. I decided to leave the gang, so now I got to face up to everything that comes my way. People have to make these kinds of decisions. If they want to stay and feel sorry because they know that they're not going nowhere, well, that's for them to decide. I made my decision not to stay because that's not what I wanted to do the rest of my life."

For others departure to places outside of Chicago represents the way of seeking an escape from gang participation. Elf and Tony indicated having left for New Jersey and Puerto Rico, respectively, only to return several months later.

Elf was sixteen years of age when he left the Diamonds and moved away from Chicago. "I have family there [in New Jersey] who are related to my father. One uncle told me to come down, that he could find me a job in construction. It didn't work. He told me that the corporation had hired already all of the day labor they needed. Day labor is the people who do the dirty work, cleaning the construction site and stuff like that. So after several months I came back, and the guys took me back. I didn't beg or anything, and I didn't tell them a bunch of lies about where I had gone to live and the kind of job I had. The chief knew that I was really upset with the way that things have been going lately. He gave me a raise of a couple of dollars, and I came back to work. But you know what? As soon as I can get a decent job, I'm gone. And they can kiss it good-bye."

Tony went to live in Puerto Rico, where he remained for more than a year. "I liked the island," he told me. "That was lots of fun. But you know what? There are as many gangs there as here. A lot of parents send their kids over there to get away from the problems of the streets here, but those problems are there, too. I was going to stay, but there were people from the opposition over there, so I split. You know, I left to get away from all this bullshit around here—you know, the selling, getting busted, and then the whole cycle again. That gets old after a while. So, I went to Puerto Rico. It's not like my parents sent me there. I told them that I wanted to go and get away from the streets. Of course, they were delighted. So my father called my grandparents, and they took me in. This was the first time I lived with them. My other grandparents are here, and I've been around them all of my life, but with these folks it was different. It took some time to get used to each other. They wanted to treat me like a child—like, I couldn't go out at particular times or stuff like that. Anyway, when things got hot over there I came back and got violated real good. I was beat up something fierce, but you know what? Like, I didn't give a fuck. I figure it works both ways. I went on my own, I had a good time, and now I had to pay for it.

Manny, a young man who was always talking about designing buildings, signed up for the military. This was his strategy for escaping the suffering of gang participation. Manny was a very shy young man. The few times that we talked he behaved quietly and reserved, making only occasional remarks. On the day I learned about his decision to join the military he was in a relatively friendly mood and appeared to be jubilant, speaking excitedly about his decision. He agreed to come to my university on a Saturday to talk. On the way there we talked mostly about his family, but once we were in my office he only wanted to talk about the marines.

Manny: I took the test for the marines, and I'm going after the summer. I want to have a little bit of fun before I go. So, they let me stay until then.

Felix: And what about the guys—what are they going to say when they find out that you're leaving them?

Manny: I think that my clique, the guys out on the street—like, there is a group of four or five of us guys who are really tight—well, you know, it's not going to be the same. In fact, I'm trying to talk one of them into coming with me. He and I go back to elementary school.

Felix: What about the mainheads—what are they going to say to you?

Manny: I don't think that they are going to be too uptight about it. In our last meeting they were talking about too many people talking about wanting to get their V-out and stuff like that. But I have a legitimate excuse; it's not like I'm going to join another gang.

Felix: And what made you decide to go into the marines?

Manny: Well, I've been talking to my mother about it for some time. She doesn't want to see me hanging out, and I think I've gotten tired of it, too. Just the other day, for nothing, we got busted. So, if we are getting busted for nothing, if we are not making no money, . . . I mean, like, look at me, I don't have no money. I can't even buy me a hot dog right now. So, if nothing is happening with being in the gang, why not look to do something constructive? At one point, hey, I was ready to give everything for what we were doing. But you learn that only a couple of guys are getting rich from your work, while you are sleeping in jail or spending long hours in jail for nothing. For nothing. But one thing that I will not do is let those guys beat me up. Hey, I've given them too much already. So, I'm going to walk out without them putting me through that—that's bullshit.

Felix: But what do you think is going to be the difference between the marines and the gang?

Manny: Like I told you, right now I don't have anything. At least when you come out of the marines or even the army you have something. People look at you in a different way. They show respect for you. Let's say that I decide to go to college. Well, I can get college benefits. Maybe I'll do that. I can't do anything right now.

The decision to develop forms of resistance against the Diamonds is a very difficult one for most youngsters. After all, it was through the Diamonds that they were able to salvage a sense of self-worth and dignity. And in the process they developed intimate familial relations and a strong affirmation of their ethnic ties and solidarity. To leave their friends behind would mean a major violation of the code of family loyalty. At the same time the actions of some members of the Diamonds to resist and renegotiate their parts in the system and rules imposed by the mainheads are a clear indication of the active struggle to which these youngsters are committed in their quest for achieving life goals. Their keen sense of justice will not allow them to accept domination, the logic of defeat and exploitation.

This chapter has examined the cyclical life patterns of members of the Diamonds. The discussion has shown how these young men have traveled a road leading back to its very starting point. It is quite likely that at the end of the journey they are even more disadvantaged than when they first began. At first the attitudes of Coco, Benjy, Flaco, Lobo, and the others toward conventional work were very negative. These young men indicated not wanting to get involved in jobs in the regular economy, which they had defined as oppressive. As they spent more and more time working for the Diamonds, these young people began to observe how their organization, the very same mechanism that was expected to serve as their liberator from the tyranny of conventional work, had fastened them into a position of subordination.

The members of the Diamonds I spoke to became aware over time of the oppressive nature of the gang and, in doing so, decided to take action toward their liberation. Their decision was to resign from the Diamonds—a very difficult and painful resolution given the attachment they had developed to each other. Although they are aware of how conventional society responds to those bearing a deviant label, members of the Diamonds have not given up. They are taking their chances in the hope that new opportunities are given to them. Will this every happen? If so, will these young men realize success with so many odds set against them?

Conclusion

The story of the Diamonds is just one of many involving young people in U.S. society today who at an early age were removed from normal paths to the attainment of a quality life and throughout their adolescent years were stigmatized and treated like deviants and criminals. Fully aware of their fate, these young people turned to their smaller community and appropriated elements of their Puerto Rican culture and ethnicity to organize themselves into a cohesive organization through which to plan and negotiate their life chances. Youngsters' conscious understandings of the workings of social institutions, as limited as that understanding might appear, joined with their heavy reliance on ethnic and cultural elements to make their experiences as members of the Diamonds quite unique. In turn, the realities of labor exploitation and oppression they suffered as members of the Diamonds's work force prompted them to separate from the organization. This response also contributes to the uniqueness of the Diamonds, for there is a popular view that suggests that "once a gang member, always a gang member." Members of the Diamonds made the decision to resist further oppression by resigning from the organization and reentering conventional society in a continuing search for a way of life that would improve their conditions.

Indeed, the willingness on the part of members of the Diamonds to "make something of themselves" offers hope to their chances of finding reliable opportunities. The real challenge facing these youngsters as well as others wanting to improve their life chances is: How does one retranslate what has been a failure of confidence throughout one's life into confidence in a new reality, permitting youngsters to find outlets for their high aspirations?

— Looking Ahead

In writing the story of the Diamonds I came to know a group of youngsters who, like my own university students, are in dire need of securing fundamental working knowledge for achieving specific life goals and ambitions that is current, accurate, and functional. Unlike my university students, who are already proficient at following up on leads provided by professors, counselors, and other university staff personnel, members of the Diamonds lack the skills needed to gain access to conventional social roles. For those interested in working with youngsters like the Diamonds it is imperative to recognize that these individuals must be outfitted with practical information and introduced to individuals willing to guide them.

My experience with members of the Diamonds has shown me that the process of enhancing their circumstances requires that significant others become engaged in their lives, actively participating in a process of interaction and communication through which assistance is provided for helping them to achieve a restoration of confidence and the faith needed to fight off the many internal and external threats that stand in the way of social and economic advancement. Since these youngsters have been deprived of the concern and involvement of influential individuals, it is little wonder that they feel an enormous amount of confusion and frustration as they struggle to make sense of themselves as individuals and to improve their socioeconomic conditions. As some of the Diamond's put it, "I want to, but I don't know how. There's no one there to help us."

It is clear from the various accounts provided by these young men that they have developed some ideas about particular activities they feel competent in carrying out; they are not convinced, however, that the doors of opportunity will be opened and willing to receive them. And in those rare cases when they manage to convince themselves that, indeed, there is a small opening through which they can squeeze, there remains the fear that persons inside will not be understanding and compassionate about their past circumstances.

I recall meeting Rey for the first time and feeling so impressed by his knowledge about the field of architecture. We were driving to my office to conduct an interview on one occasion when he began pointing out some things he found to be inaccurate with the architectural designs of some buildings we passed along the way. He told me that he had been interested in architecture for a long time, having taken some courses in high school which exposed him to some of the fundamental elements of the craft. When I asked him why he did not pursue this career he answered, "To do that you need a high school diploma and then college. Which college is going to take me? And then, you know, those teachers in college, they are as bad as the ones I had in high school. That's why I quit in the first place. They don't care for you. Since I don't talk like a college student, do you think they will ever try to help me? I'm not going to give them the chance to mess with my mind no more. Hey, how many more times do we need to be put down?"

Clearly, the accumulated negative experiences that members of the Diamonds have received in their educational journeys and from contact with the police and other adults in general have instilled in them a distasteful picture of conventional society. This long and frustrating history of negative experiences cannot be erased overnight simply by providing them with lectures and sermons on the virtues of conventional life. Nor will speeches about their deviant behavior influence them to rethink and reorganize their lives. These young people need to be convinced that, indeed, there exists an alternative to what they presently are doing; they also need to be shown the clear and direct road leading to its fulfillment.

There is no denying that a great deal of gangbanging goes on in Suburbia and that the Diamonds are key players. It is also true that gangbanging produces great physical injury and, at times, death to children and young and old people. Certainly, at times, some of the victims are innocent bystanders. But to condemn it outright is to ignore the larger historical process through which this aggressive behavior emerged. Gangbanging is a specific consequence of the business being carried out by the gang because its members have been shut off from society's legitimate economic sector. It is important not to be lured into a view of members of the Diamonds as psychopaths and hard-core criminals who do not care for their lives or those of others and who refuse to accept assistance when it is offered by conventionally "successful" persons (a typical argument is that they simply do not want to "straighten out"). Such a view, in my opinion, misses the mark completely. I would argue, in fact, that, unless we look closely at the development of the business gang—and especially at how the enterprise of drug dealing is linked to a lack of job opportunities and openings for Latino youngsters within the conventional economy—we cannot hope to understand this ethnic entrepreneurial creation or how to establish alternatives to it.

In addition, it is hoped that we, as individuals functioning in mainstream society, take the necessary time to understand the youngsters' historical journeys of emotional attacks, severe pain, failures, and contradictions and how these relate to their decisions to join the gang. If we proceed along these lines, we are likely to discover, specifically, that many individuals, regulations, and activities of social institutions—and particular forces and conditions existing within and outside the youngsters' immediate social environment—have contributed immensely to gang participation and its accompanying forms of behavior, considered deviant by conventional standards. Another discovery we might make is that for members of the Diamonds, gang participation has come to represent a way of insulating themselves from the negative judgments people have made about them as individuals over time. Gang participation, in short, provides these youngsters with a context in which some semblance of self-respect and dignity can be maintained.

Thus, if we are truly concerned about the human rights of gang members and if we are committed to doing something to improve their socioeconomic circumstances, we then must agree to take a comprehensive look at their life journeys: their historical backgrounds, their circumstances within the gang, and their future aspirations. This is no small task, for it requires individuals to spend long periods of time with the youngsters in an ongoing human relationship. Through this kind of "extended period of interaction" these young people will come to witness our commitment to understanding their world as they see it—in particular, understanding why they view the gang as the most rational response to their social and economic circumstances. It seems to me that this is the least we can do for a group of youngsters who, correctly so, share the view that society has abandoned them, who feel that the adult world wants absolutely nothing to do with them with the exception of helping to get them arrested and put them behind bars.

As I indicated at the beginning of the book, in conducting my study I did not set out to provide a romantic portrayal of the lives of members of the Diamonds so that the larger society could see them as more humane than they really are or feel sympathy for them. I am convinced that I have accomplished my original task by reporting the information provided by these youngsters. That I was impressed and at times shocked by what I discovered cannot be denied. Witnessing the enormous amount of hope still being carried in the eyes, minds, and hearts of these young people after so many years of constant emotional abuse has further encouraged and solidified my commitment and sense of responsibility to our youth. My work has given me an opportunity to witness the remarkable abilities and desires on the part of these youngsters to survive a very difficult moment in our nation's history and their persistent struggles to pursue and accomplish the "American dream of success." I am convinced that these young people must be provided with the necessary nurturing to become integral components of the resource base that is essential if we hope to have progressive change and a better society.

I do not agree with the idea that we must treat these youngsters as if they were our enemies. In fact, this we/they dichotomy used to define relations between the conventional world and gangs must give way to a whole new interpretation built around dialectical affiliation—people working together to eradicate common experiences of inequality and injustice. The efforts must be geared to meeting the needs and wishes of every neighborhood resident. In particular, we need to come together as one people to ensure that all of our youngsters are emotionally and intellectually empowered by those institutions of society whose responsibilities include, among other things, helping young people through the very difficult phase of adolescence.

Reference List

Adler, Patricia A., and Peter Adler. 1980. The irony of secrecy in the drug world. *Urban Life* 8:447–465.

Becker, Howard. 1963. *Outsiders*. New York: Free Press.

Berry, Brian J., Irving Cutler, Edwin H. Draine, Ying-cheng Kiang, Thomas R. Tocalis, and Pierce de Vise. *Chicago: Transformation of an Urban System*. Cambridge, Mass.: Ballinger.

Carey, James T. 1968. *The Drug Scene*. Englewood Cliffs, N.J.: Prentice-Hall.

Chicago House Hunt Book. 1989. *Logan Square*. Chicago: Meyers and Associates.

Chicago Tribune. 1988 (May 26). Dreams, and little else, go with eighth graders. Sec. 1, col. 5.

City of Chicago, Department of City Planning. 1958. Development plan for the central area of Chicago. Unpublished report.

———. 1989. Life along the boulevard." Unpublished report.

Cloward, Richard, and Lloyd Ohlin. 1960. *Delinguency and Opportunity*. Glencoe, Ill.: Free Press.

Cobas, Jose. 1987. On the study of ethnic enterprise. *Sociological Perspective* 30, no. 4: 467–472.

Cohen, Albert. 1985. *Delinquent Boys*. Glencoe, Ill.: Free Press.

Cummings, Scott, ed. 1980. *Self-Help in America*. Port Washington, N.Y.: Kennikat.

Eitzen, Stanley D., and Maxine Baca Zinn. 1989. The forces reshaping

America. In *The Reshaping of America,* ed. Stanley D. Eitzen and Maxine Baca Zinn, 1–13. Englewood Cliffs, N.J.: Prentice-Hall.

Fusfield, Daniel R., and Timothy Bates. 1984. *The Political Economy of the Urban Ghetto.* Carbondale, Ill.: Southern Illinois University Press.

Giroux, Henry A. 1983. Theories of reproduction and resistance in the new sociology of education: A critical analysis. *Harvard Educational Review* 53, no. 3 :257–293.

Goffman, Erving. 1963. *Stigma: Notes on the Management of Spoiled Identity.* Englewood Cliffs, N.J.: Prentice-Hall.

Hagedorn, John M. 1988. *People and Folks: Gangs, Crime and the Underclass in a Rustbelt City.* Chicago; Lake View Press.

Hicklin, Charles, and Wendy Wintermute. 1989. The employment potential of Chicago's service industries. Unpublished manuscript.

Hispanic Housing Development Corporation. 1989. Building communities—rebuilding Chicago. Unpublished report.

Horowitz, Ruth. 1983. *Honor and the American Dream* (New Brunswick, N.J.: Rutgers University Press).

Kornblum, William. 1987. Ganging together: Helping gangs go straight. *Social Issues and Health Review* 2:99–104.

Kornblum, William, and Terry Williams. 1985. *Growing Up Poor.* Lexington, Mass.: Lexington Books.

Latino Institute. 1983. *Latinos in Metropolitan Chicago: A Study of Housing and Employment.* Chicago: Latino Institute Publication, Monograph #6.

Light, Ivan, and Edna Bonacich. 1988. *Immigrant Entrepreneurs.* Berkeley; University of California Press.

Merton, Robert K. 1957. *Social Theory and Social Structure.* Glencoe, Ill.: Free Press.

Miller, Walter. 1969. Lower class culture as a generating milieu of gang delinquency. In *Delinquency, Crime, and Social Process.* In ed. Donald R. Cressey and David A. Ward, New York: Harper and Row. 332–348.

———. 1974. American youth gangs: Past and present. In *Current Perspectives on Criminal Behavior,* 291–320. ed. Abraham Blumberg, New York: Alfred A. Knopf.

Moore, Joan. 1978. *Homeboys: Gangs, Drugs, and Prison in the Barrios of Los Angeles.* Philadelphia: Temple University Press.

Padilla, Felix M. 1985. *Latino Ethnic Consciousness.* Notre Dame, Ind.: University of Notre Dame Press.

———. 1987. *Puerto Rican Chicago.* Notre Dame, Ind.: University of Notre Dame Press.

Sullivan, Mercer L. 1989. *Getting Paid: Youth Crime and Work in the Inner City.* Ithaca, N.Y.: Cornell University Press.

Taylor, Carl. 1990. *Dangerous Society.* East Lansing: Michigan State University Press.

Thrasher, Frederick L. 1927. *The Gang.* Chicago: University of Chicago Press.

United States Bureau of the Census. 1930–1980. *Characteristics of Population.* Washington, D.C.: Government Printing Office.

Vigil, James Diego. 1988. *Barrio Gangs: Street Life and Identity in Southern California* Austin: University of Texas Press.

Williams, Terry. 1989. *Cocaine Kids.* Reading, Mass.: Addison-Wesley.

Wilson, William J. 1980. *The Declining Significance of Race.* Chicago: University of Chicago Press.

Index

193

omy, 38; teachers, 6, 71–76;
worsening, 28. *See also* school
Eitzen, Stanley D., and Maxine
Baca Zinn, 38
empowerment, 23
ethnic background, of gang members. 19. *See also* gang
ethnic business enterprise, gang
as, 8, 14, 103–109. *See also* gang
ethnic solidarity, as gang ideology, 14, 107
ethnographic research, 17
exploitation, by gang, 6

family, as gang ideology, 6, 104–
106. *See also* gang
Fusfield, Daniel R., and Timothy
Bates, 34
future aspirations, 156–167; career, 159; educational
attainment, 158; and fear of failure, 159–161; going legit, 157,
158

gang: activities of, 16, 22; affiliation, 7, 8, 11, 12, 13, 19; as a
business enterprise, 13, 14, 15,
21, 92, 103; control of hoods
and markets, 16, 20; control of
schools, 40; as counter organization, 103; crews and group
types, 4; as a criminal operation, 13, 21; cultural and
economic characteristics, 13;
cultural and ethnic characteristics, 14; cultural symbols of, 2, 3;
customers and clientele of, 15;
dominant culture explanation
of, 5; domination in, 6; drug
dealing, 48; emotional support
of, 24; as an employer, 13, 14; as
an ethnic enterprise, 14, 104–
109; exit from, 4, 78, 179, 180;
exploition in, 6; family ideology
of, 6, 104–106; group solidarity,
107; harassment of peer group,
65; identity, 27; inequality in, 6;

joining, 78–80; limitations of,
153; mobility in, 12; money-
raising capacity of, 113–116; occupation structure in, 13, 111;
opposition or enemy gangs, 13,
26, 27; participation, 2, 4–6, 8, 9,
21; positive views of, 6, 9, 23, 66–
68; protection, 6; Puerto Rican,
14; relationship with customers,
110, 111; reputation, 7; research
about, 4; sections of, 2, 3, 16;
school influence of, 79; signals
and symbols, 66; social and cultural characteristics, 104–109;
socialization, 13; survival in, 9;
turning, 55; violation rituals, 55–
60
gang banging, 10, 21, 60–63
gang members: disillusionment
with gang, 162–167; ethnic
background, 19; as ethnic entrepreneurs, 3; families of, 10; fear
of failure, 159–161; former, 12–
15, 17; future hopes of, 156–162;
gaining self-respect, 9; girlfriends of, 7, 14; as hired labor,
5; life of, 13; mothers of, 7, 8; Pee
Wees or Littles, 113–121; perception of conventional work,
101; as psychopaths, 9; roles of,
5; seniors, 114; skills of, 153–155;
stigmatization of, 27

Giroux, Henry A., 5
Goffman, Erving, 22
going legit, 157, 158
graffiti art, 2, 27

Hagedorn, John, 3, 4
hanging out, 2, 7, 9, 22, 25, 27
Hicklin, Charles, and Wendy
Wintermute, 36, 38
Hispanic Housing Development
Corporation, 45, 46
historical approach, 5
hoods, 7, 27
Horowitz, Ruth, 102, 103